THREE ROADS SOUTH

Search for a Latin American Cultural Identity

Copyright © 2002 by
University Press of America,® Inc.
4720 Boston Way
Lanham, Maryland 20706
UPA Acquisitions Department (301) 459-3366

PO Box 317
Oxford
OX2 9RU, UK

ISBN 0-7618-2446-4 (paperback : alk. ppr.)

⊖™ The paper used in this publication meets the minimum
requirements of American National Standard for Information
Sciences—Permanence of Paper for Printed Library Materials,
ANSI Z39.48—1984

To my wife Ana María, to our children, José Ignacio, María Inés, Juan Francisco, and Rodrigo Eduardo for the love they have for their two cultures, and to my son Stephen René for not forgetting the language of his birth

Contents

Foreword

I suppose that all of us who teach carry with us the image of one or two of our own professors who more than any of their peers influenced us in the decision to pursue an academic career. Whatever the source of our admiration may be, from scholarly erudition, to wonderful organization skills, or simply a passion to communicate new concepts and to share knowledge, we are deeply grateful to have been given a model that would become forever a guiding source of inspiration for us.

I am one of many who had the good fortune to learn from Professor Lloyd Hulse in the cozy environment of classrooms at Lewis and Clark College. We learned from him the basics of grammar, vocabulary, and reading strategies, and took to heart high expectations of dignity and mutual respect as the essence of an unwritten code of conduct in class. More importantly, however, was that he embodied what he taught and shared with his students: the best of the values of the two cultural worlds in which he lived.

We who were lucky enough to have Professor Hulse as our instructor and counselor for an overseas study program in Peru often observed that being able to communicate well was a function not only of language but also culture. All of us came to appreciate, sometimes with more than a little embarrassment, how different structural combinations and cultural contexts could change the meaning of even the most familiar words and phrases!

At times we enjoyed the special treat of listening to our professor sing to his own guitar accompaniment. The beauty and gracefulness of his rendition of "La malagueña," and the plaintive laments of "La barca de oro" expressed feelings that one could understand even without knowing a word of Spanish.

When Professor Hulse spoke with us about cultural differences between the United States and Latin America, he did so from the perspective of an American who had acquired linguistic skills and cultural viewpoints through years of living and working in Latin

America. Husband and father in a bicultural bilingual family, he experienced the culture that was still foreign to us, even to those of us who had taken advantage of the opportunity to study abroad.

Three Roads South: Search for a Latin American Cultural Identity is a book in which Professor Hulse shares his understanding of Latin American culture. He does this especially well when he compares his experiences in Latin America to his upbringing as an Anglo (a term that I do not recall him using, but one that I quickly learned when I arrived in Albuquerque to do my doctoral studies at the University of New Mexico). This concise volume provides a general overview on the question of Latin American unity and complements well such excellent books as Floyd Merrell's *Sobre las culturas y civilizaciones latinoamericanas,* and *The Latin Americans: Understanding Their Legacy,* by Randall Hansis.

In his chapter on the unifying features of Latin American culture, Dr. Hulse personalizes them through various anecdotes, and by referring to his own experience. He explains in detail certain themes of special interest, such as "personalism and verbalism," "the role of women, family," and "social classes." The section of the book on the importance of rhetorical skills reminds me of my surprise during evening entertainment in Mexico, when in addition to the traditional fare of song and dance, local orators would share the stage to mesmerize their audiences by the dramatic and often emotional recitation of selected poems. In the early days of American television this was done on variety shows, such as the Ed Sullivan Show, but I can hardly imagine such a thing today.

Professor Hulse's final chapter, although brief, offers one of the most useful and colorful description of *gringo* stereotypes I have ever seen. I have always been a *gringo* (in Mexico, and also Peru, but not in Argentina!), but I did not realize the quantity and variety of *gringos* that are commonly perceived. American students of all ages and backgrounds will benefit from a better understanding of how their behavior and dress might fit into one or more of the stereotypical categories.

I mentioned earlier the books by Merrell and Hansis. Their volumes, written primarily for college students, are similar in that they propose to communicate to their readers what they need to know about Latin American culture to be able to understand it. Lloyd Hulse is less ambitious in the sense that he does not try to paint his pictures with the same wide brush as his colleagues. What he does share with us is the fruit of many years of work and study, plus plenty of objective and personal experience: objective as professor of Spanish and its cultural milieu, and personal as an English-speaking American who became completely bilingual and bicultural. The author's own careful translation of the elegant prose in Spanish of his original *Tres caminos hacia el sur* will be used by students, travelers, and those who are interested in cross-cultural communication and related issues.

His book *Three Roads South* takes us along on a pleasant trip that enriches the reader in both cultural and linguistic terms. For one of his former students, it is an opportunity to become acquainted once again with a mentor and a friend.

Bradley A. Shaw
Associate Professor of Spanish
Kansas State University

Preface

Three Roads South: Search for a Latin American Cultural Identity is the translation of *Tres caminos hacia el sur,* published in October 2000. The present English edition is prompted by the interest of people who wanted to read the original edition, but who do not know Spanish.

Three Roads South, just as its predecessor, offers three approaches to Latin America. The first one highlights its ethnic and geographical diversity, and is obliged to present a few basic facts, such as the number of countries, their names, location, and the predominant ethnic composition of each. Several mnemonic classifications follow, to help the reader relate one country to another, for example, their type of government, industrial development, and literacy level.

With this background, together with a few facts given in passing, one begins to examine the causes of Latin America's political and socioeconomic divisions, among which formidable geographic barriers play a role, not to mention what for many is the economic and cultural imperialism of the United States. Then begins a discussion of the problems faced when trying to integrate the diverse indigenous populations and subcultures into a cultural and socioeconomic mainstream. To complement this discussion I have added personal observations over socioeconomic discrepancies and cultural contrasts from many years ago, which are as surprising as those of today.

The second approach, the antithesis of the first, explores in depth the common values that constitute Latin America's mainstream culture. Among the experiences that have forged these values are found the cultural identity provided by language (Spanish or Portuguese), uniting people of different socioeconomic levels and ethnic groups, the cultural patterns handed down by Roman Catholicism, the search for a Latin American identity frequently juxtaposed to that of the U.S., the mark of a disproportionate and overwhelming geography, the inclusion of Indians by the Church in the colonial hierarchy, which began a process of racial mixing (*mestizaje*) with the result that today most Latin Americans are *mestizos*, nominally Catholic, and speak Spanish or

Portuguese. Noted are the following cultural traits: *personalism* (with its complement *verbalism*), the historical influence of the extended family, the special role of women, aristocratic attitudes and class distinctions, people's pride in their shrewdness, and distrust of official stories and policies, the use of language to attack, dissimulate, and create the appearance of reality, which at the same time is a mask and a barrier.

The third approach, totally new, based almost exclusively on my own bicultural experience, seeks to synthesize the first two approaches, by bringing the values and contrasts discussed earlier into sharper focus through an analysis of mutual Latin and Anglo-American stereotypes, which come from underlying cultural values. More attention is given to the stereotypes of the *gringo* than to those of the *Latino*, because the purpose of the last approach is to highlight Latin American cultural values and show Anglo-Americans how the former see them.

Three Roads South, which I myself have translated from *Tres caminos hacia el sur,* not only comes from my research as a university professor on the culture and literature of Latin America, but also from what I have lived. I have wanted to express my opinions, reflections, and feelings, because they come from what I have experienced intimately: the living experiences of a young man from the north, who went south to perfect a language that had fascinated him, and to be a part of another culture long before becoming a university professor.

Fifty-four years ago I traveled from La Grande, Oregon to Mexico City by bus, with the purpose of getting to speak Spanish like a native. I stayed there for more than four years. First, I lived with a family, just like the Lewis and Clark College students who participated in study programs that I have taken to Latin America. The difference is that my home stay did not come as the result of arrangements made beforehand by a university, or other organization, but from the spontaneous invitation of a young Mexican man from a well-to-do family, who was traveling on the same bus. Later I studied at Mexico City College (now the University of the Americas), where I received my master's degree after interrupting my studies to work a year in rural Mexico as a livestock inspector.

As a result of these experiences and later ones, again in Mexico and twelve other countries, without counting the constant reference during forty-two years, to the point of view of my Salvadorian wife, I have felt the need, even the obligation to intersperse in this book a personal anecdote, or two, if relevant.

Three Roads South is a hybrid, academic and personal at the same time. It does not lack the support of reliable sources, although the date of some is not recent. However, they serve the purpose of supporting the exploration and analysis of the topics and cultural contrasts presented.

The sources that I have read and researched support what I have lived and observed. My intention in this book is not so much to contribute the latest data, or delve into historical details. For that there are many other books. Mine, on the other hand, sets out to explore and analyze Latin America's cultural values at length, taking advantage of my bicultural and personal perspective. This perspective provides implicit, as well as explicit bicultural contrasts, almost from the beginning of the book. Therefore, this book may prove interesting to Latin American readers (once they skip past the basic facts of the first pages), as well as North American university students like the ones who participated in my classes, or who accompanied me to Latin America in the academic programs I was privileged to direct.

During my career as a professor, which lasted some twenty five years, I unconsciously expected my students to show the same enthusiasm for the language and culture that I felt. I seldom saw my expectations realized, but on a few occasions I did see that enthusiasm flourish, as happened in the case of Brad Shaw.

Bradley A. Shaw, the author of the prologue, went with me to Peru in 1965 in a study program. Afterwards, he obtained his doctorate in Spanish and has been a professor at Kansas State University for many years. Without his help, which goes back to 1995, this book would not have been published. He has read the manuscript many times, and through long correspondence has given me many valid bits of advice. I owe him my most heartfelt thanks.

I also owe thanks to Professor José Promis of the University of Arizona for his advice and the trouble he took, without any obligation, to read and comment on my original manuscript. Thanks go also to Salvador Velazco, who was a professor of literature at Lewis and Clark College for a year. I thank John McCelland III, my *compadre*, as well as my colleagues at Lewis and Clark College, in particular Vance Savage, who read and commented on the original manuscript in its early phases. I also wish to thank Larry A. Meyers, Director of Overseas and Off-Campus Programs for sending *Tres caminos hacia el sur* to Professor Lynn Hirschkind in Ecuador, who after reading it expressed her interest in adopting the translation for the next Lewis and Clark Program in Cuenca.

To my wife Ana María I owe my most special thanks for the many hours that she has devoted to helping me with this book, including the idea of suggesting to me the original title *Tres caminos hacia el sur.* From this suggestion, coupled with recent advice from my son Francisco to use the word *south* adverbially, comes *Three Roads South* as the main title of this English edition. Finally, I thank everyone who directly, or indirectly, has helped me in my endeavor.

Chapter One

The Variety of Latin America

Countries and Inhabitants

Anyone who sets out to write about Latin America faces an overwhelming, though fascinating task, because of the variety of its inhabitants, who speak not only Spanish and Portuguese, but perhaps also Nahuatl, Otomí, Tarascan, Mayan, Quiché, Aymara, Quichua (or Quechua), and Guaraní. Ranging in complexion from white to dark through gradations of light to dark olive skin, even black, without absolute racial identification, many of its inhabitants live in cities larger than New York, or London. Others live in rural villages under conditions similar to those of centuries ago, except for the transistor radio, or maybe a television antenna on the housetop of the local leader.

In addition to the great ethnic variety of the inhabitants (linguistic also, if we consider the survival of indigenous groups still unassimilated into the mainstream culture), the superlatives of Latin America's geography astound and overwhelm us. Examples are the height and breadth of the Andes Mountains, the extent of the scorching Atacama Desert, the interminable sinuosity of the Amazon River, with all its tributaries. Crawling like a serpent through thick, impenetrable jungles, it is filled with trees yet unclassified, a veritable kingdom of an inexhaustible abundance and variety of flora and fauna.

Like many other texts on Latin America that stress its differences, this first chapter sets out to give a background of basic information, which, together with later valuations, may guide the reader. This person may be an advanced student of Spanish (or Portuguese) who wants to understand better the culture in which the language is nourished, or a Latin American residing in the United States who wants to understand aspects of Anglo-Saxon culture that differ from his/her own.

Taking a panoramic approach to Latin America from the outside obligates the writer to stress its variety. This is a necessary step in order to understand it, but the number of aspects presented can cause an erroneous impression, if one chooses only one of these aspects as being representative. An example might be the impression left with North American readers about Central America by the Life World Library book, published in 1964. They must think that Central America is an area populated by Indians and poor peasants, without large cities or people dressed in Occidental clothes.[1] A lady from El Salvador—of the formerly wealthy aristocracy—vehemently objected to the fact that this book did not at all represent her people and her culture, including those who identify with them, who are often members of the underprivileged classes. In the early 60's, when a high school student from a small town in Oregon asked this same lady how the people in El Salvador dressed—thinking perhaps of the indigenous dress shown on the cover of above mentioned book—she answered indignantly, "Better than you!"

A Guatemalan university professor of leftist ideology also does not identify with the Indians from Santiago de Atitlán, shown on the previously mentioned book cover clothed in short stripped pants. According to him, some of the customs of the Indians of his country, including their typical dress, often not of pre-Hispanic origin, were imposed by the Spaniards, and then by their descendants, the *criollos*, during the Colonial period. Therefore, preserving these customs keeps the Indians subjugated, and the achievement of their rights will not be fully realized until they adopt Western dress.[2]

---

[1] Harold Lavine, *Central America* (New York: Time Incorporated, 1964).

[2] Severo Martínez Peláez, "La cuestión de la cultura del indio," *La patria del criollo* (2a. ed., San José, Costa Rica: Editorial Universitaria Centroamericana, EDUCA, 1973), pp. 594-618.

From the above it is obvious that if we are to optimize communication, or intercultural understanding between the United States and Latin America, it is very important for U.S. citizens, above all, to know which Latin Americans are their interlocutors.

The variety of Latin America relates to these questions and also to the problems within each country, to those of each country with its neighbors, and finally to the problems of each, or all of them, with the United States and the world. Thus we must take into account the undeniable variety of Latin America, a vast area perennially troubled by divisive forces, problematic, though extremely interesting, an area in many ways as exotic as India or Morocco.

The numerous countries of Latin America, 20, including Haiti and Brazil, reveal divisive forces that impede its progress. Even without the plethora of problems it faces, the sheer presence of so many national borders, perpetuates problems both inside and outside the region. The inconvenience of so many national borders between small countries is experienced acutely by anyone traveling by car through Central America. One will most likely have to go through customs and immigration three times in the same day, which stand between countries whose inhabitants speak the same language, have the same customs, have the same ancestors—Indians and Spaniards—and the same type of government. These borders seem as arbitrary as if one were to set up an office of immigration and customs between Oregon and California, and another between this state and Nevada. In fact there are agricultural control stations where one does not have to wait for hours to have passport and bags checked, rather only a moment to say that one is not carrying any fruits or vegetables.

Classification of the Latin American Countries

According to their geographical position, the countries are generally grouped from north to south, and from west to east, as follows: Mexico, Central America, with the five countries that originally constituted the Central American Union—Guatemala, El Salvador, Honduras, Nicaragua, and Costa Rica—plus Panama, which was part of Colombia until 1903. Next comes the northern part of South America and the Caribbean: Colombia, Venezuela, Cuba, the Dominican Republic and Haiti. (The last country is not Spanish speaking. In its place one should count Puerto Rico, which is Spanish speaking, but normally excluded from the 20 countries because of its special relationship with the United

States, as a Free Associated State.) Then come the Andean countries: Ecuador, Peru, Bolivia and Chile (although this last country is different in some aspects), followed by those of the River Plate: Argentina, Uruguay, Paraguay and Brazil. The last one is included, because some of its streams flow into the Paraná, Paraguay, Uruguay, and Pilcomayo rivers, which come together in the River Plate (*Río de la Plata*).[3]

Ethnic differences will be treated in greater depth later. For the moment, without going into detail, it is sufficient to group the countries according to their ethnic composition. The countries that are considered to be predominantly *mestizo* are Mexico, El Salvador, Honduras, Nicaragua, Colombia, Venezuela, Chile and Paraguay. Indians predominate numerically in Guatemala, Ecuador, Peru and Bolivia. Blacks are evident, together with a *mestizo* population in Cuba, Panama and the Dominican Republic. There are also blacks in the coastal areas of Honduras, Nicaragua, Colombia, Costa Rica and Venezuela. The population of Haiti is almost entirely black. Brazil does not lend itself to an easy classification, but one could say that in the Northeast a black population is evident, together with *mestizos* of all types. In the interior a *mestizo* population predominates, in which one notes more indigenous influence. In the states of the South, for example, in São Paulo, Paraná, and Rio Grande do Sul, the population is more European, or white, like those of Uruguay and Argentina. Costa Rica is also classified as a white country, the same as the countries of the River Plate.[4]

The inclusion of Costa Rica in the list of countries with a European population is accurate with regard to the Valle Central, without taking into account regions like Guanacaste, which has a largely *mestizo* population. Also, not to be forgotten are the blacks from Limón, descendants of the Jamaicans who came to work on the banana plantations of the Atlantic coast. And in the capital, San José, during visits that took place between 1959 and 1994, I have noticed more and more the presence of *mestizos*.

One thing is the ethnic classification, and quite another, people's attitudes regarding their ancestry, which is sometimes taken lightly, as shown in the following popular joke: "They say that the Mexicans are descendants of the Aztecs, the Peruvians of the Incas, and the

---

[3] Hubert Clinton Herring, *A History of Latin America* (3rd. ed., New York: Alfred A. Knopf, 1968), p. 147.

[4] Herring, p. 16.

Argentines are all descendants of ships." They tell another one, which goes as follows: "The Argentines are descendants of the Italians, speak Spanish, live in French style houses, and consider themselves English." The business of considering themselves English must trouble them now after the Falklands' War, or the War of the Malvinas. However, popular jokes retain some element of truth. In this case, as in others, no matter how slight: "It's the truth that hurts." Consequently, in this regard I should not fail to mention the following. The other day while reading Borges, the thought suddenly struck me that this Argentine, of so much renown, was really an Englishman at heart, except that he expressed himself in impeccable Spanish.

To understand the problems of Latin America other classifications are useful. One classification, summarized below, and based on theatrical centers, is valuable in that it reveals literary nuclei and the countries they cover. They are Mexico City (Mexico and Central America); Havana, before the Castro Revolution (Cuba, the Dominican Republic, and Puerto Rico); Caracas and Bogotá (Venezuela and Colombia); Lima (Peru, Ecuador and Bolivia); Santiago (Chile); Montevideo and Buenos Aires (Argentina, Uruguay y Paraguay).[5]

The above classification makes clear that certain countries are culturally dependent on others. For example, it reveals that the Central American countries depend on Mexico, and that Paraguay depends on the large cities of Buenos Aires and Montevideo. It emphasizes the high literary level and isolation of Chile, separated from Peru to the North by the Atacama Desert, facing the sea, and with its back to the Andes and Argentina on the other side. Chile is isolated by its narrow, elongated shape and its geographical position, aside from the disputes it has had over bordering lands with its Trans-Andean neighbor, which increase its isolation. Although crossing the Andes today is not the great feat once faced by San Martin's troops, the nearest Argentine cities, such as Mendoza, are still far from Buenos Aires, the literary center of the neighboring country.

Following are other classifications, which together with the above, help one to understand the complex reality of the countries and inhabitants of Latin America:

---

[5] José Juan Arróm, *Certidumbre de América* (2a. ed., Madrid: Editorial Gredos, S.A., 1971), pp. 215-22.

1) Countries with the most industrial development: Mexico, Argentina, Brazil, Colombia, and Venezuela and Chile in the last decades

2) Countries relatively free of dictatorships: Mexico, although according to many it had a party dictatorship until the PRI lost power, Costa Rica (Chile and Uruguay up until the 70's, later democratic once more), Colombia and Venezuela in the last decades

3) Countries in which agrarian reforms have been undertaken: Cuba, Mexico, Bolivia, Peru, Guatemala, Nicaragua, and

4) Countries with the highest literacy: Argentina, Uruguay, Chile, Cuba, Costa Rica and Nicaragua.

Historical, Social, Geographic, and Economic Divisiveness

The influence of historical and social factors in the disunion of Hispanic America is hard to evaluate. Many writers refer to the political breakup after Independence as the result of inadequate political experience, due to the fact that during the Colonial period the most important government posts were in the hands of Spaniards from the Iberian Peninsula. Although this is true, it is useful to examine for a moment the character of the Spaniard himself, in order to reach conclusions that may help to trace a connection with historical events.

Spaniards are constantly inclined to cultural and political separatism, a tendency evidenced today by the Basques and the Catalonians, aside from the well-known regionalism of Galicia and León. A Latin American writer refers to the separatism of the Spanish people, as follows: "In that same territory, united by the name Hispania, uniformity does not exist with regard to the composition of its people."[6] He points to the multiethnic composition of Spain itself: Iberians, Celts, Phoenicians, Carthaginians, Romans, Germanic groups, Arabs, Jews, and Gypsies. Another writer, the Spanish philosopher, José Ortega y Gasset, in his *España invertebrada,* maintains the thesis that the separatism of the Spaniard, or *particularism*, begins with the Spaniard himself. Each man is his own political party. [7]

---

[6] José Agustín Balseiro, *Expresión de Hispanoamérica* (San Juan, 1960), p. 11. (The translation from Spanish is mine.)

[7] (2a. ed., revisada y aumentada, Madrid: Espasa Calpe, 1922), passim.

In spite of the apparent unity of the Spanish Colonial Empire, one cannot conceive of it in terms of modern nations, such as the United States, France, England, or Germany. Scholars rush to point out that Spain transplanted in the Americas a feudal society, which found fertile ground to take root and perpetuate itself in a land occupied by stratified indigenous societies that simply changed masters. Moreover, Spain's Counter-Reformation with its strict control of traffic to the Colonies impeded the arrival of currents of European thought until the Colonial society had taken firm root. After Independence the social structure did not change substantially, in spite of idealistic efforts to establish a union. The social hierarchy remained resistant to change. It was a hierarchy initiated at the end of the Reconquest by the *Conquistadores*, a warrior class with a feudal mentality, which under the system of the *encomienda*, received large land grants with Indians to work on them.

The question arises as to whether land holdings today— characterized in many countries by *latifundios* (very large properties of the few) and *minifundios* (extremely small properties of the many)— plus landless peasants, are not partly due to the *encomienda*.

After separation from Spain, what caused the failure of idealistic attempts to achieve political union and carry out hoped-for social changes? To the causes mentioned earlier, in addition to not facing the Colonial structure of land holdings until the late 20th Century, I would add another. It is a strongly rooted cultural trait, a *hierarchy of loyalties*, which affirms above all the value of the person: "I come first," "Long may I live!" and Don Quijote's "I know who I am." Intertwined with this affirmation comes loyalty to the family: "Charity begins at home." Then comes love of one's own region, the *patria chica*, and only after that comes duty to the nation. One tends to feel loyalty toward persons or one's *patria chica*, sooner than toward abstract systems. The region is often governed by a strong person, the *caudillo*, in one sense, the descendant of the *conquistador*, who normally does not interfere in the loyalties of the Latin American toward himself, his family, other persons, and his region, or *patria chica*.

The idealistic efforts of Latin Americans to unite were frustrated by their *hierarchy of loyalties* and their political inexperience, plus the feudalistic Colonial socioeconomic system that still prevailed. These factors in turn must be linked to the realities of Latin America's geography, mainly physical barriers and distances, in addition to the influence of the *central* powers (the industrialized nations) and the problem of large indigenous groups that have not yet been assimilated into the cultural and economic mainstream of their countries.

Geography alone has isolated one country from another, and to a certain degree, has isolated both from abroad. It has also isolated the inhabitants within the same country from each other, as is the case of the residents of Iquitos in Peru, who in the past could travel more easily to Europe than to Lima, the capital. On one hand, nature has been extremely kind to Latin America. Kind, for example, in providing a mild climate for most of the capital cities. Lima, Peru, in spite of its latitude and sea level location, enjoys a good climate, which would be very hot if not tempered by the Antarctic marine current. At the beginning of the Colonial period, sites at high altitudes were chosen for the majority of the capitals, thus avoiding extremes in temperature. On the other hand, nature has been cruel in its geography of physical barriers—mountains, jungles, and deserts—which have created a kind of *archipelago*.[8] The Andes extend along the length of South America, varying in height from 6,069 to 22,309 feet (1850 to 6800 m), and reaching a width of up to 403 miles (650 km). In addition there are the lesser mountain ranges of South America and their continuation through Central America and Mexico, where they join with the Rocky Mountains in the United States.[9] As for jungles, the Amazon, together with the barrier created by the Andes, links cities such as Iquitos, Peru more with Brazil and the jungle areas of Ecuador than with Peru itself. The Darien jungle between Panama City and Colombia is a barrier across which land transportation is not feasible. With regard to deserts, the Atacama Desert, mentioned earlier, is a formidable barrier that extends some 1798 miles (2900 km) the length of Chile's northern coast and the greater part of Peru's coast. There are also deserts in Argentina, Mexico and Brazil.[10]

Partly because of these barriers, the population centers of Latin America appear like islands scattered along the coastal strips, or like communities isolated in the mountains until the advent of air transportation. But this convenience is not available to many, who cannot pay for an airplane ticket, or buy an automobile. Their economic means only allow them to travel by land: on foot, horseback, or on the

---

[8] Eduardo Galeano, *Open Veins of Latin America* (New York and London: Monthly Review Press, 1973), p. 281.

[9] Herring, p. 6.

[10] Herring, p. 11.

back of a mule, when they cannot take buses, which in some places can only travel during the dry season. Public land transportation is not sufficient in most parts of Latin America, because of the inadequate development of highways and railroads. An example is Peru, which does not have a highway for automobiles and buses that extends the entire length of the country.

Besides the barriers mentioned above, without considering the immensity of the Atlantic ocean, Spanish regulation of commercial routes until the end of the Colonial period isolated certain areas. Furthermore, although in the following story of the handkerchief, logic finally prevailed, one must ask if members of the wealthy class still today have not abandoned their custom of importing luxury items, even those of necessity, instead of manufacturing them locally. The lace handkerchief, before being sold and given as a gift to a lady of Peru's viceregal court, has to cross the Atlantic as raw material, cotton, from Portobello to Seville. From there it is sold in the same form to a Flemish agent, who sends it by sea to the place of manufacture. On the way back, now in the form of an embroidered handkerchief, it arrives in Seville, then crosses the ocean again to Portobello, from there crosses the Isthmus to Panama City, from where it is shipped to Callao and again sent by land to its final destination.[11]

Latin America's demographic distribution, which is affected by geography, as well as by many economic factors, perpetuates its divisions, aptly described by the term *archipelago*. Areas of more than ten persons per square mile (2.6 km.^{2}) are separated by others that are sparsely populated, as is the case in Yucatán, whose inhabited areas are separated from the rest of Mexico by a swampy coastal belt where very few people live. In a similar way, the populated regions of Central America are separated from the northern part of South America by the Darien jungle, just as the strip of land that forms Chile, unequally populated itself, is separated from Brazil and the River Plate countries (Argentina, Uruguay, Paraguay) by the Andes, as was mentioned before.

Regionalism is intensified by another factor. The inhabited areas in the mountains are small relative to the number of people, that is, they are more densely populated than the coasts, yet are still isolated from

---

[11] Herring, pp. 188-200.

each other.[12] This factor, combined with the difficulties of transportation in the mountains, economic problems, plus the regionalist mentality of the inhabitants, intensifies Latin America's divisions.

A few economic factors, such as mere distances, aggravate the problem. The economic integration of Latin America would require more exchange of goods between one country and another. However, until now most of the traffic takes place between individual Latin American countries and North America, or between them and Europe, in the same way that transportation of goods over great distances now is done across the United States. One reason for the relatively little exchange of goods between Latin American countries in comparison with the exchange carried out with North America or Europe, lies in the fact that in Latin America the average distance between settlements of 10,000 inhabitants each, is two and a half times greater than in the United States.[13]

Distances and the earlier mentioned geographical barriers hamper the development of unpopulated, but promising areas, such as the *montaña* of Peru, the Eastern slope of the Andes. The problem in developing this zone in particular is due to the lack of means of communication and the difficulties in getting plants and animals to adapt to a totally new environment. With regard to the economic development of the large populations already established in the mountains, perhaps distances and terrain are the greatest obstacle.[14]

Latin America's economic difficulties can be illustrated more by comparing it with the United States with regard to combinations of arable land and rainfall.

Latin America has its fruitful plains, producing grains and pasturing cattle. But they are meager compared with the United States' broad expanse of level lands between the Appalachians and the Rockies . . . This disadvantage is coupled with the land tenure problem. The problem of lack of rainfall is

---

[12] J. P. Cole, *Latin America: An Economic and Social Geography* (London: Butterworths, 1970), pp. 14-15; p.52.

[13] Cole, pp. 22-23.

[14] Cole, p. 59. "Perhaps more seriously for the economic development of the countries with large highland population (in Guatemala--unassimilated Indians) than difficulties with plant and animal adaptation is the cost added to transportation."

evidenced for example in Mexico, Brazil, Peru, Chile . . . or there is too much. The Amazon is not the farmland of the future.[15]

Today more than ever this last statement is substantiated by the deforestation of the Amazon.

Latin America's disadvantage with regard to agriculture is intensified by the practice in the majority of the countries of growing non-edible crops: cotton, coffee, tobacco, and henequen, not to mention coca, for foreign currency. Frequently, to the detriment of the poor, some of this currency has to be used to import expensive foodstuffs. Members of the oligarchy, owners of *latifundios* (large landholdings) among other things, have taken advantage of this type of agriculture, and have little incentive to modernize. The above mentioned practice is combined with landholder absenteeism, a subordinate peon class, and the necessity of getting foreign currency (be it to import consumer items, for industrialization, or reforms), besides the frequent embezzlement of subsoil riches and the problem of indigenous groups that live outside the monetary economy, not to speak of the generalized ideal of avoiding manual labor. This combination of factors, intertwined in varying ways and intensities, coupled with the so-called imperialism of the United States and other industrialized nations, has caused Latin America's intellectuals to think that the solution is revolution. However, where there have been revolutions, in Cuba, for example, one can ask if the successes compensate for the failures. Granting the material benefits—or rather the supposed equitable distribution of what there is—Cuba survives thanks to its sugar cane, the same as before. Although everyone eats, certain foods are rationed, and the country depended on the subsidy from Russia, which has ended. Castro has spoken of the *zero alternative*, and it would seem that due to his charisma, or out of spite, some Cubans adhere to the revolutionary path, no matter how many turns it has taken. Under socialism Cuba did not industrialize. The same as before the Revolution, it sells its sugar cane for foreign currency, and continues to import foodstuffs.

Because of the economic difficulties discussed above, many people who are concerned about Latin America, whether they are

---

[15] I have been unable to ascertain the source of the above text (in English, according to my original notes), but it is not Powelson, *Latin America: Today's Economic and Social Revolution* (New York: Mac Graw Hill, 1964), p. 36; p. 44, as indicated in the first printing of *Tres caminos hacia el sur*.

revolutionaries or simply reformers agree on the need for drastic and authoritarian measures. Rather, one should say that this has been the attitude until the recent return to *democracy*, condemned by the leftist revolutionaries as a "tool of imperialistic capitalism." Let us say that in the last few years, the reforms attempted by many Latin American nations—not only from the left, but also from the right—have had the goal of advancing on three fronts: industrialization, agrarian reform, and freedom from the economic domination of the industrialized countries through alliances with other countries of the third world. The industrialization that has occurred has been achieved at a high cost: an external debt, or an "eternal" one, as embittered jokers say. Moreover, agrarian reform has been seen to be economically unfeasible, according to people of different ideologies, as well as its victims, and dependency seems greater than ever. Paying the interest alone on the external debt exhausts the foreign exchange currency of some countries. Thus, no matter what one's point of view may be, at present there is less agreement and optimism regarding the solution of Latin America's economic problems.

Ethnic Variety, Subcultures and Problems of Integration

The tremendous variety of Latin America, both from the negative point of view of its socioeconomic problems, as well as the positive one of its cultural richness, can be stressed by treating in greater depth its ethnic composition. Let us see some points of view, together with statistics.

In spite of numerous indigenous groups in Mexico (7.5 - 30%), in Guatemala (40 - 60%), Ecuador (15 - 20%), Bolivia (40 - 60%), and Peru (25%), in general the *mestizo* predominates numerically.[16] That is why the Mexican intellectual, José Vasconcelos, considered him the *new man* of Latin America, the promise of the future.[17]

Contrasted with this *promise of the future,* is the predominate socioeconomic and cultural diversity of Latin America, which is

---

[16] Tim Guldiman, Lateinamerika: *Die Entwicklung der Unterentwicklung* (Munich: Verlag C. H. Beck, 1975), p. 7.

[17] José Vasconcelos, *La raza cósmica* (Paris: Agencia Mundial de Librería), p. 192, passim.

underscored in the following classification of its inhabitants in nine cultural types:

1) tribal Indians 2) modern Indians 3) peasants (*mestizos, cholos, ladinos, caboclos*) 4) sugar refinery - plantation workers 5) factory - plantation workers 6) urban dwellers 7) members of the metropolitan upper class 8) members of the metropolitan middle class 9) the urban proletariat.[18]

The problems of social integration seem insurmountable in Latin America. Integration of the Indian in the socioeconomic mainstream, whether possible, desirable, or inevitable, is an unresolved question that worries many, from writers to revolutionaries. The following literary works, to mention just a few, reflect the changes in attitude over the years toward the Indian: *Tabaré, Cumandá, Aves sin nido, Raza de bronce, El indio, Huasipungo, El mundo es ancho y ajeno, Todas las sangres* y *Redoble por Rancas*. Bloodthirsty warrior and cannibal, innocent child, noble savage free of the evil influences of civilization, beast of burden, what was the Indian? Did he have a soul? Even if he had, was he still not like a child in need of protection, similar to that given to him by the Jesuit Order in South America? Many sociologists of the 19th Century saw the Indians as a subjugated mass that was a burden for the countries they inhabited, and who had to be integrated and absorbed into larger populations of *superior* European immigrants.

Still today many North American tourists see the Latin American Indian as picturesque, poor, but contented. Some tourists, and most of the university students from the United States, who are worried about social justice, believe that the Indian should vindicate himself without ceasing to be an Indian, since, in general, anthropologists besides North American and European historians exalt his pre-Columbian past and continue to condemn the Iberian Conquest and Colonization. Likewise, the Conquest is condemned in Mexico. Since the Revolution, the governing party (until recently the PRI, or Institutional Revolutionary Party) has exalted the Indian as a national hero in the figure of Cuauhtemoc. Mexicans pride themselves on there being so many statues of him, and none of Hernán Cortés. In this there is a lot of rhetoric, but one can also detect sincere attitudes on the part of many people, and the integration of many features of the indigenous past have been appreciated and truly incorporated in the national folklore.

---

[18] Robert J. Havighurst et al., *La sociedad y la educación en América Latina* (Buenos Aires: Editorial Universitaria de Buenos Aires, 1962), p. 66.

Mexico has taken positive steps in this sense, perhaps more than other countries. However, it should be noted that aside from history books, the Ballet Folklórico, and museums, in actual everyday life, the Indian gets ahead more by becoming a *mestizo*.

Whether condemned or exalted, in the majority of cases throughout history, the Indian has been a victim: of the *Conquistadores*, the *encomenderos* (those granted control over land and Indians), the owners of mines and mills, the generals, the politicians, and even of the Jesuits and the revolutionaries. An escape that many Indians have used is to become cultural *mestizos*. This way they can be integrated in the Hispanic mainstream (or in the Brazilian mainstream in the case of tribal Indians), and eventually better their position in society. A Guatemalan professor describes how this process begins in his country:

> It is well understood that the Indian who dresses in canvas and wears boots is no longer an Indian. And he is less so, if together with Spanish he speaks other modern languages. And he is even less of an Indian, if he replaces his religious brotherhood with the union and the 'temascal' with antibiotics, and if he throws away his plaintive flute and bares his throat in order to sing out songs of proud confidence in himself. [19]

Today, in spite of the partial progress achieved in Mexico, and recommended in Guatemala, negative attitudes persist in everyday life. Let it be noted that the vindication for the Indian recommended by the Guatemalan professor (of leftist ideology) is for him to cease to be one. Although he blames the Colonial period for what it was, his recommendation reveals a realistic, though negative assessment, just like the warning given to North Americans in Ecuador, which they branded as racist. It was not racist, but rather cultural. "Watch out for Ecuadorian motorists when you cross the street; as pedestrians, we are all Indians." Or the question one is asked in El Salvador after one has had an outburst of ill humor. "Have you got over acting like an Indian?"

From what has been expressed above regarding the problem of integrating the numerous indigenous groups, which, according to some, will have to cease to exist as such, it can be inferred that it is more of a

---

[19] Martínez Peláez, p. 611. (The translation from Spanish is mine.) One day in one of my classes this same explanation was totally rejected by several students, who refused to understand the use of the term *Indian* in a cultural, instead of a racial sense.

cultural, rather than a racial question. With this statement, I do not mean that there is no racial prejudice. Of course there is, in Latin America as well as in other parts of the world. As for the preservation of indigenous customs, I imagine some will be lost in the reality of everyday Latin America, but I hope that the desirable elements of the Indians will be preserved in the *mestizo* culture, as it has been done in Mexico.

The problem of social integration is more than a cultural question, and it concerns a great many people, mostly *mestizos*. It stems mainly from the enormous economic discrepancies that hinder integration, and above all social justice. One of these discrepancies is unequal pay for a day's work. I remember that when I worked in 1950 with a Mexican partner in a rural area of Mexico, my salary was very high in comparison with his.[20] He received a total of $35 *pesos* per day, and I $45, just for expenses, besides my salary of $265 dollars—equivalent to $2518 *pesos* per month, or $84 per day—plus $100 dollars ($950 *pesos*) each month to rent an apartment. This discrepancy was not justified, but its origin can be explained in part by the difference between the two national currencies. In the sector we worked, agricultural laborers (*peons*) earned only $3 *pesos* per day, less than one tenth of what my partner earned. The Mexican cavalry soldiers who at times escorted us on our routes earned barely a few more *pesos*, and on several occasions they were present when right before them the paymaster would give us quantities of money—in cash—which represented more than a year of their salary. My partner and I thought on more than one occasion, that instead of protecting us, the soldiers could have taken the money from us and headed for the bordering state of Guerrero, well known as a refuge for outlaws. To the peasant leader, a *comisario*, at whose table we sat down to eat on one occasion, the quantity we received must have seemed fabulous, or perhaps incomprehensible.

Examples of extreme socioeconomic differences abound, such as the slums of the poor who have just arrived, poverty belts around large cities with houses built from tin and cardboard. They contrast with the skyscrapers and ostentatious monuments honoring *revolutions* and *leaders*. Donkey and mule trains plod along dirt trails, while jet planes

---

[20] This was in the Joint U.S. – Mexican Campaign to Eradicate Hoof and Mouth Disease in which I was an employee of the U.S. Department of Agriculture (with a GS-7 rating).

streak through the sky at supersonic speeds. Known abroad are the most difficult and experimental novels, written for other novelists (like themselves), who for the most part are sophisticated, well traveled, and often residents in Europe, while many semiliterate people in their countries read photoromances and comic strips. Known abroad are cosmopolitan diplomats and erudite professors, in contrast with peasant leaders who do not travel, such as the *comisario* mentioned above, who did not seem to have a clear idea of Mexico as a nation, when he referred to what he did not know as "those lands out there." For him, my Mexican working partner, born in another state, was just as much an outsider (*fuereño*) as I. Both of us were from "those lands out there."

Not all contrasts are problematic. In its variety Latin America offers a cultural richness that has fascinated both travelers and scholars. The structural changes that are necessary to reduce the abuses of human rights must be made without destroying this richness. Concern for the poor is justified in Latin America. Certainly they are not "happy natives," as can be seen by the number of Latin Americans who arrive in the United States to escape economic hardship, as well as violence. Statistics on *per capita* income are a cause for concern; however, they need to be corrected in light of what is known about the income of two thirds of the population, consisting of many indigenous groups and peasants not integrated into the monetary economy. In addition there is a very large informal sector, whose earnings are not counted in the statistics. Moreover, the demands of many Latin Americans—justified, on the other hand—must be seen against the backdrop of expectations for a better life. These expectations come not only from the media, but also from socioeconomic improvements themselves, which are real in many countries if they are viewed in the long run. The logical result of these improvements is to expect, even demand that they continue.

Latin America's diversity and its problems of socioeconomic and cultural integration are aggravated by the tendency—understandable in light of the area's history—for many people to seek solutions from abroad, or in the embodiment of authority in one person. Paternalism was cultivated during the Colonial period, when authority, as well as political and economic control, came from the *conquistadores*, the holders of *encomiendas* (control over land and Indians), the royal inspectors, and finally from the viceroy, the direct representative of the crown, and his rival, the archbishop. The result of this is today's large landholder, the *hacienda* or *estancia* owner, the military leader, or the charismatic strong man, the *caudillo*, as well as the industrial entrepreneur and the exporter who flaunt their economic power, which comes from their contacts abroad. Now the United States and the international conglomerates constitute what is abroad, or *outside*, for most Latin American countries. The exceptions are Cuba and Nicaragua, although the United States continues to exercise its power in these countries.

Many Latin Americans alternately tend to blame and then praise countries abroad, due to their concept of how authority works, a concept formed by the Colonial authorities and maintained by their modern counterpart. The authorities from within ultimately receive their power from *outside*, and people turn to them on personal terms. Solutions are sought through personal contacts, which gravitate outward, in a centrifugal manner. One turns first to family members, then friends. The next step is to take advantage of an influential *compadre*, the godfather of a son or a daughter. Finally, to solve problems there are the *caudillo*, the colonel, or the general, followed by the president, or dictator, of the country, who handles things with the authorities abroad, such as John Kennedy, and Ronald Reagan in years past, more recently George Bush, Sr. As examples of the *caudillo* who manages affairs with leaders from *outside* we still have Fidel Castro, and not too long ago Manuel Noriega and Daniel Ortega as heroes for many Latin Americans because—as persons—they challenged the president of the United States.[21]

As the result of a lightning attack, condemned in Latin America less than one expected—*A lo hecho, pecho* (What's done is done)—Manuel Noriega ended up as a prisoner in Florida. Daniel Ortega, in command of the Sandinistas, came to form part of the democratic opposition, because he allowed elections to take place, though it is a recourse in which he really does not believe, and to which he acceded only for the moment. He went along with the elections in the first place, because he expected to win, as everyone predicted, including the Spanish-speaking observers of Univisión.

On the other hand, Fidel Castro—the stagnated *caudillo* of socialism, who in the name of his ideology was willing to take his people to the "zero alternative" —challenged Bush from the "museum" of his regime, proclaiming that "capitalism was the "museum," since it was older. He continues to cling to his ideology, though with some

---

[21] A Salvadorian professional residing in Canada, who was exiled because of his socialist ideology, protested my including Manuel Noriega in the list of "heroes." As I recall, he did not think that the inclusion of Fidel Castro was erroneous.

signs of realism. Castro's Revolution now must *taste* bad to him, like the *cheese* the *baturro* bought (*baturro*: peasant from Aragón, known for being stubborn).[22]

---

[22] The *baturro* goes into a store and asks the storekeeper to sell him "*that cheese.*" "Don José, that isn't cheese, but soap." Don José continues to insist that he sell him "*that cheese*," and after a long while the owner gets fed up and sells it to him. Four days later the *baturro* comes back to the storekeeper complaining that the *cheese* he sold to him tasted like *soap*.

Chapter Two

The Cultural Unity of Latin America

Language and Religion

In light of the previous chapter, which stressed the variety of Latin America, now it will seem paradoxical to speak of its unity. However, the aim of the current chapter is to explore the common values that make up its cultural mainstream. To undertake this task it is necessary to treat first the obvious common denominators of language and religion, which have served as a basis to differentiate Catholic Latin America from Protestant Anglo-America. Language and religion have been the main components in defining the term *Latin America*, which comprises the countries of the Western Hemisphere whose official language, Spanish, Portuguese, or French, is derived from Latin, and whose religion is Roman Catholic. Added to this definition is the geographical component of being located to the south of the United States. Thus, the mainly French speaking Province of Quebec is excluded only because of its location. On the other hand, Haiti, which is officially French speaking and borders on the Dominican Republic, is usually included in books on Latin America. However, it will be excluded from the present study, because it seems to me that most Latin Americans, with the possible exception of Brazilians from the Northeast, do not view Haitians as part of their cultural identity. Likewise, French Guyana, one of the three European enclaves on the northeast coast of South America is excluded, as are the Caribbean islands of Martinique and Guadeloupe, which, moreover, are parts of Metropolitan France. Remaining are the Spanish-speaking countries, including Puerto Rico, and Portuguese-speaking Brazil, normally considered part of Latin America.

At times, in the discussions that follow, it will be necessary to differentiate *Hispanic America* from *Luso-Brazilian America,* both of which are parts of *Latin America.* Besides, it should be noted that at times the term *Latin America* is often used imprecisely to refer to *Hispanic America.* In fact, I have observed that Brazilians use the term *Latin America* to distinguish themselves from Hispanic Americans. A precise term for the area treated in this study would be *Iberoamerica,* but I prefer the customary *Latin America,* which in its use places us firmly in the New World. Also for many readers the latter term takes into account the influence of France as a mentor for Latin American intellectuals during the 18th and 19th centuries.

The attitudes of Latin Americans toward the Spanish and Portuguese they speak, as opposed to the Spanish and Portuguese of Spain and Portugal, constitute a strong unifying force. In spite of noticeable national and regional differences, they are proud of speaking Spanish and Portuguese to each other in a manner revealing fewer differences than those perceived between themselves and the inhabitants of Spain and Portugal. They feel that their version of Spanish and Portuguese incorporates the experiences of the New World, as opposed to Old. Even though they are different languages, there is a common ground between Spanish and Portuguese in mutually intelligible references to the flora and fauna of Latin America, aside from their common vocabulary and similar grammatical structures. In fact, they are so similar that one fails to appreciate enough some really important differences between them.

Spanish is especially important as a unifying cultural factor for Hispanic Americans, who in spite of coming from so many different countries, recognize and appreciate the bond created by speaking the same language, which entails, as does every language, an infinite number of cultural implications. Brazilian Portuguese, though it does not serve the purpose of establishing a link between the inhabitants of different countries, covers an enormous area, and offers a Brazilian identity to very different peoples and regions.

While providing a cultural identity, the influence of American Spanish and Portuguese is strengthened through their surprising uniformity, especially if one considers the extension and variety of the regions in which they are spoken by more than five hundred million persons of extremely different ethnic origins and socioeconomic circumstances.[1] At this moment it is not necessary to start a detailed description of the linguistic features that differentiate Latin American Spanish and Portuguese from their peninsular counterparts. Suffice it to say that they have their own physiognomy, whose main features reveal the experience of Latin Americans, giving them a vehicle of communication and identification that first links them to one another, and only then to Spain and Portugal. Moreover, their language is the factor that separates them the most from Anglo-Americans, and gives them, even when they are living in the United States, a notable cultural resistance.

With regard to unassimilated subcultures in the United States Octavio Paz writes that the most evident one is that of the Chicanos, whose resistance is not only sociopolitical, but also cultural.[2] The Chicanos are an example of an Hispanic American minority group living in the United States, whose cultural resistance is partly due to the preservation of their Spanish, despite the influence of English and their habit of switching back and forth between English and Spanish. As for the Hispanic population in the United States in general, I believe that in the last few decades, immigration from Cuba, Central America, as well as Mexico and elsewhere, without forgetting the influence of the media in Spanish, has reinforced the continuation of its cultural traditions, which is due mainly to the more frequent and consistent use of Spanish.

On many occasions I have observed the way Latin Americans from different countries, as well as ethnic origin, identify with each other, particularly when they meet among non-Latin people. The following anecdote will serve as an example. Some years ago, when bringing up the topic of Latin American cultural unity with a lady from El Salvador, I alluded to her feeling more in common with a friend of hers from Mexico than with a Bolivian woman, with whom, to be sure, she had had less contact and had known for a shorter time. Nevertheless, she identified more with her friend from Mexico because of class and ethnic origin. Furthermore, her Mexican friend was not a "newcomer" to the upper class, as was the latter. However, when I asked the Salvadorian if something linked her to the Bolivian (because I had

---

[1] Oxford Analytica, *Latin America in Perspective* (Boston: Houghton Mifflin Company, 1991), p. 5

[2] "México y Estados Unidos: posiciones y contraposiciones," *Vuelta*, No. 27, v. 3, febrero de 1979, p. 7.

observed their holding long conversations on several occasions), her answer was very clear: "the language, of course."

The following quotation sums up the points made about language as a cohesive force, in contrast with the variety and diversity of Latin America, emphasized in the first chapter:

> Let us take away from Latin America that network of linguistic complicities, and we will have an archipelago, geographically disconnected, economically disintegrated, socially torn, politically Balkanized, an easy prey for all imperialisms. Let us intensify the consciousness of cultural unity, and from it we will attain the remaining unities. Contemporary history has demonstrated fully that imperial violence cannot sever with the sword what the Word has joined. It is demonstrating this today in Latin America."[3]

From the secular point of view of the late 20th century, one would be tempted to discount the importance of religion in connection with the cultural unity of Latin America, beyond the fact that Spain and Portugal imposed Roman Catholicism on their colonies. It is frequently said today that most Latin Americans are Catholics only *through habit*, that few go to mass, especially men, many of whom (aside from obligatory attendance during childhood) can be found in church, so it is said, only three times in their life: at their own baptism, their wedding, and their funeral. Despite the fact that even now, women go to mass more frequently and in greater numbers than men, in general the influence of the Catholic Church is less evident than it was at the end of the 19th century, when in most Latin American countries its power was weakened due to the rise of liberal regimes. Even if one accepts that the influence of the Catholic Church was greater in the past, its teachings have left cultural patterns, ideals, ways of thinking and acting that prevail subconsciously until now, to the point that even non-practicing Catholics who join evangelical sects continue to have many beliefs and attitudes that do not change. The following quotation about Protestant Latin American women is an example:

> Although women spend many hours reading the Bible—a sacred activity for evangelical Christians—and asking God to keep them away from the

---

[3] Luis Brito García, "La unidad de lo real y lo imaginario," *Casa de las Américas*, 28: 166, ene-feb., 1988, p 115. (The translation from Spanish is mine.)

world, they engage in the same activities as women who are not of that religion. For example, it is common in Mexico and Central America to say to the husband "mi señor" [equivalent to my lord, or master, in this context], with all the connotations that this implies in our societies.[4]

The latent influence of Roman Catholicism in Latin America, and its legacy, are exemplified en the following quotation taken from an article about the Pope's visit to the Hemispheric Conference of Bishops in Puebla, Mexico, towards the end of the 1970's:

> One should not forget that Catholicism (and within Roman Catholicism, the Pope) is communication for Catholics, though they be, as they often are, Catholics only in a cultural sense.[5]

The continuing importance of religion in Latin America is evident in the sociopolitical implications of *Liberation Theology*, a movement which arose after the Second Vatican Council in the early 1960's and the Conference of Bishops in Medellín, Colombia in 1968. It arose as a reaction of young priests, who wanted to resolve the sociopolitical and economic structures that perpetuate poverty in Latin America. The Pope, conscious of these implications in a predominantly Catholic continent, visited the Conference in Puebla to resolve theological divisions within the Catholic hierarchy. The Pope again visited Latin America in 1985 and 1989, where he, with the exception of Nicaragua (1985), was warmly received by large and enthusiastic multitudes. The Pope's difficulties in Nicaragua sprang from his strong criticism of the *Popular Church*, supported by the *Sandinistas* with Marxist leanings who were then in power, as well as from his disapproval and condemnation of priests in cabinet level governmental positions.[6]

In 1985 I attended a mass officiated by the priest heading the *Popular Church,* who, standing in front of a mural that equated the guerrillas with Christ, gave a sermon severely criticizing the anti-*Sandinista* clergy, such as Father Carballo. The music was provided by a professional group of musicians. The small congregation at that mass

---

[4] Berta Vargas, "Cristianas protestantes en América Latina, "V.S. No 20, Ene.1982, p 87. (The translation from Spanish is mine.)

[5] Jean Meyer, "El viaje del Papa," *Vuelta*, No 27, v. 3, Feb-1979, p. 49. (The translation from Spanish is mine.)

[6] Penny Lernoux, People of God (New York: Viking Penguin Inc., 1989) p. 98.

consisted mostly of North American and European reporters and photographers. A few "normal citizens" were present, of whom some, no doubt, were Nicaraguans. One could argue that the lack of parishioners was due to the day and the hour, but it is strange that a few days later, the 29th of April of the same year, I attended a traditional mass officiated by Father Carballo-Bismark. That day the church was filled with Nicaraguans from every social and economic class. On May 1, 1985, I was again able to observe hundreds of people, poor for the most part, coming out from a mass that had officiated by the highest prelate of Catholic Church in Nicaragua, Monsignor Obando y Bravo. They were on their way to participate in an anti-*Sandinista* demonstration, which they said "was going to be broken up by government mobs (*turbas*)." They were asking all us foreigners present to witness how they would fare. In fact, the large, unhappy crowd was dispersed by a well-disciplined platoon of *Sandinista* soldiers.

According to Father Carballo-Bismark, the *Popular Church*, started during Salvador Allende's presidency in Chile by the movement *Christians for Socialism,* was a totally Marxist political ideology, which the *Sandinistas* were using for the benefit of the revolution. The name had been changed to *Popular Church* to give it a more easily acceptable image, since the word *Socialist* was strongly rejected. Father Carballo made a distinction between the *Popular Church* and *Liberation Theology*, which was still under scrutiny, and which, as such, should remain open to many suggestions, to avoid making the mistake of confusing it with Marxism.[7]

A measure of the influence of the Church in Latin America is the affirmation that it is "the last and only source of justice for the poor."[8] There is an obvious connection between the Church, accused previously by many of being the traditional ally of the élites, and the search for social justice in Latin America. Many priests of all hierarchies hold that social justice demands a total commitment to protecting the poor, regardless of political implications, whether Marxist or not. On the other hand, many like Father Carballo, in agreement with the Pope's concerns, fear the political implications of *Liberation Theology,* based on Marxist socioeconomic analysis, which considers capitalism to be the cause of unjust social structures,

---

[7] From a recorded interview with Father Carballo, after the mass of April 29, 1985.

[8] Lernoux, p. 96.

"institutionalized violence" or "social sin," recognized, as well as perpetuated, by the "trappings of a formal democracy that would not alter the desperate poverty of the people."[9]

At this moment I do not intend to pronounce judgement on matters concerning the position of the Catholic Church regarding *Liberation Theology,* nor its politicization in the hands of the left. Neither do I intend to mention various evangelical churches that support in different ways this *Theology,* used to nurture the goals of the *Sandinista* revolution in Nicaragua and those of the guerrilla movement in El Salvador. The use by the left of *Liberation Theology's* premises has been met with violence from the right. This violence, just as any other, should be condemned, but at the moment we cannot debate its causes. The point I want to make here is the cultural importance of religion in its main form, Latin American Catholicism, before attempting to describe facets of its cultural legacy in more detail.

The importance of the Church, past and present, allows for political structures to be altered without having to change cultural patterns, as affirmed below:

> The appeal of liberation theology in Latin America lies in its integration of religious and political liberation: If religion previously served as a repressive political tool, it can also be used as a means of political liberation. In other cultures it is not always easy to find such a perfect match of religion with politics, but in Latin America Catholicism is the cultural starting point for everything else, the one element that unites peoples with different languages and historical experiences. Latin Americans do not have to change their basic religious beliefs—their culture—to achieve liberation, but only their perspective.[10]

I agree with connecting politics, religion and culture and to a certain degree with the assertion that the basic religious beliefs of Latin Americans do not have to change in order to alter political structures.

---

[9] Lernoux, pp. 94-96.

[10] Lernoux, p 98. While translating into English the original Spanish edition of this book, *Tres caminos hacia el sur,* I discovered a wording mistake in the comment following this quotation, which should have read: "creencias *religiosas* básicas," not "*políticas.*"

Certainly one has seen a radical political change in Cuba, without a basic change in the mutual attitudes of men and women. For example, many Cuban women have had to be *revolutionaries* while they continue to fulfill their traditional role of wives and mothers. And this role has been influenced greatly by the teachings of the Catholic Church. The same cultural attitudes prevail in Nicaragua, in spite of the *Sandinistas'* efforts to create a new image for women. For example, they announced that they would no longer use a woman's image, her body or face, as a "sexual object" in a commercial advertisement. This declaration seems to promise "liberation" and also coincides with Phillip Berryman's view of "liberation," quoted by Penny Lernoux. Further, in and by itself, this view is not in conflict with basic Catholic doctrine, or with the traditional roles established before capitalistic consumerism arose.

> As observed by Phillip Berryman, a popular American religious writer, liberation theology was the herald of a larger movement 'of the excluded—women, non-whites, the poor—onto the stage of history.'[11]

However, I suppose that the "larger movement" in the quotation covers much more. It would undoubtedly bring about cultural changes, if it were to be done along the lines imagined by many U.S. supporters of Liberation Theology, who do not understand the profound differences between their attitudes and the culturally determined attitudes of Latin Americans of different political beliefs. One of these differences is rooted in the way men and women see their respective roles, which are the result of the imposition of Catholicism by Spain and Portugal on millions of Indians and black Africans after the end of the struggle against the Muslims. The implantation of Catholicism coincides with the political and linguistic hegemony of the two Iberian countries and with the beginning of the struggle against Protestants. All of this happened long before the arrival of Liberation Theology. Therefore, without discounting this theology and its links to political liberation, even to women's liberation, one can conclude that from the standpoint of defining common Latin American cultural traits, the importance of religion comes mainly from the imposition of the militant Catholicism of the Counter-Reformation in the historical

---

[11] Lernoux, p. 96.

context of the New World. In other words, one must bear in mind the code of values imposed, the circumstances of its imposition, the degree to which it was achieved, and the people who received it.

Octavio Paz, upon discussing the profound cultural differences between the U.S. and Mexico, points out the implications of the Reformation in England, faced with the Counter-Reformation, whose champion was Spain. Besides, compared with the conquest and colonization of the United States, in which Indians were excluded from conversion, in Latin America the inclusion and conversion of the Indians was of utmost importance, a means of justifying the Conquest. Linking the Conquest to evangelization, as in a crusade, or holy war, is a twofold inheritance, both Catholic and Muslim, which comes from the centuries of the Reconquest.[12] The result was the biological and cultural mixing, or *mestizaje,* that left indelible marks, above all on the attitudes of men and women.

One could argue that the traditional doctrine of the Catholic Church, as well as the historical context in which it was imposed, has defined the role of women more directly than that of men, giving rise to the cultural ideal of emulating, first as virgins, then as wives and mothers, the self-sacrificing life of the Virgin Mary. Devotion to the Mother of God in Latin American Catholicism is an example of cultural mixing, or syncretism. In many cases she is simply a substitute for the feminine indigenous deities, an intermediary to whom the Indians, those of mixed blood, or the *mestizos,* as well as women, could turn.[13]

Emulation of the Virgin Mary, called *marianismo,* is considered by many the counterpart of *machismo,* the term that is used to cover the masculine attitudes of superiority and dominance over women. In the opinion of many writers *marianismo* is a repressive force, which engenders resistance to social changes, dependence, permanent submission to authority, thus perpetuating women's subjugation to men. However, one of these writers admits that women, who are subjugated by the doctrines of the Church, are its most important and numerous supporters.[14]

Not all Latin Americans have a negative assessment of *marianismo,* of the traditional cultural ideal of the role of women as wives and

---

[12] op. cit., pp. 6-7.

[13] Paz, p. 9.

[14] Leonor Aída Concha, "El poder y la mujer en la iglesia," *Fem,* v. 5, no. 20, ag., 81- ene., 82, pp. 17-18.

mothers. Many, realistically, consider it justified and necessary as a counterweight to *machismo*. Many Latin American women draw strength from their cultural ideal, from their children and their family, from each other, and from knowing that they are morally superior to men. For them this superiority is a fact, verified by the whole range of men's actions. For example, although they may not like the verbal compliment, the *piropo,* that a strange man pays them on the street, they do not necessarily feel offended, disdained, or violated, when they hear it, as do some North American women nowadays. On the contrary, they can even feel that it reconfirms their femininity, the fact that they are different, desirable and irreplaceable.[15] Latin American women acknowledge that they themselves have a role in perpetuating *machismo,* especially as mothers, by instilling in their children from early infancy, directly or indirectly, the notion of sharply different roles for girls and boys.[16] In short, in mainstream Latin American culture there is a symbiotic relationship of mutual support between *machismo* and *marianismo* that is firmly rooted in the past.

Without attempting to exhaust the vast topics of language and religion, it is now time to focus on the question of Latin American cultural unity through other topics and from other perspectives. However, one must always bear in mind that the two common denominators of language and religion have operated in combination with other factors—political, economic and ethnic—to forge a Latin American cultural identity, inversely proportional to its political and economic fragmentation.

Search for Identity: Attitudes, Ideals, Wishes and Hopes

The majority of Latin Americans realize that their initial ideal of political unity of which Bolívar dreamed during the struggle for Independence, and which Central America also sought, is unattainable. Bolívar's famous words of having "plowed the sea" are cited frequently to dramatize the futility of searching for it. However, to a degree

---

[15] A comment similar to this one was expressed in a talk given to Lewis and Clark College students on October 4, 1989 by Dr. Rosalía de Córdova, a journalist and prominent political figure in Cuenca, Ecuador.

[16] A point expressed by Dr. Arteaga de Córdova in her talk, as well as by many other Latin American women that I know.

inversely proportional to their failure to achieve political unity, many Latin Americans are aware of their cultural identity, at least as an attitude, an ideal, or wish, which is evident in many ways, frequently juxtaposed to that other, Anglo-Protestant America, the United States. There is no doubt that Latin Americans are first Mexican, Costa Ricans, Argentines, and Venezuelans, before feeling that they are Latin Americans. In the case of the Brazilians another caveat must be added. Like the Costa Ricans, or the Mexicans, they first feel that they are part of their own country, and then differentiated from the Hispanic Americans, who for them are the Latin Americans. However, once this distinction is made, the Brazilians feel a closer cultural affinity between themselves and *Latin Americans* than with *Anglo-Americans*. In turn, Hispanic Americans, who refer to themselves as Latin Americans, share a cultural affinity with the Brazilians, and include them in their Latin America, perhaps unconsciously. Brazilian *novelas* (similar, but the same as U.S. soap operas) dubbed in Spanish are shown to television viewers without their realizing—because of their cultural content—that they were not produced in Venezuela, Mexico, or Argentina. Thus it does not seem to be an erroneous generalization to include Brazil in a broader Latin American cultural context. Even so, the search for identity as an ideal, an attitude, a wish, or hope, frequently in comparison with the United States, can be seen more clearly in Hispanic America.

Many Latin Americans have alluded to a supranational identity. The following statements of José Juan Arróm give us an example. Later we can examine the list of characteristics noted by several writers that define Latin American cultural unity in a more concrete and specific way.

> Latin America is above all an area of diverse geography in which a community of peoples of undeniable cultural unity live and strive. The firm belief that we make up a single community is not new.[17]

This was the point of view of the liberators San Martín and Bolívar. José Martí, the Cuban patriot, also expressed the same concept: "from

---

[17] José Juan Arróm, *Certidumbre de América* (2a. ed., Madrid: Editorial Gredos, S.A., 1971), p. 215. (The translation from Spanish of this quotation, as well as the following, is mine.)

the Rio Grande to Patagonia we are a single people . . ."[18] Note the exclusion of the United States. Arróm contrasts the political fragmentation of Hispanic America with its cultural unity, as follows:

> Politically, it is certain, we are broken up into a handful of republics that appear on the map, as Arciniegas has pointed out, pieces of paper of different colors. But one must not be mistaken: this conglomeration of republics makes up a single historical, linguistic, and cultural community.[19]

How can one begin to define the cultural community to which Arróm refers? The dialectical connection between political fragmentation and the search for cultural identity, besides the imposing presence of the United States, in the place of the European countries —Spain, France, Germany, Russia—provide a starting point.

The political fragmentation of Hispanic America was due to the emergence of military leaders, who, representing local interests during and after Independence, supplanted the central authority of the Crown. The desire to counteract the reality of militaristic anarchy, in addition to the model of the United States as a young, independent, and democratic nation, incited the Hispanic American national heroes to pursue the ideal of a constitutionally democratic political union.

Later, as the U.S. became a dominant military and economic power, winning wars against Mexico and Spain, besides intervening with its marines in Central America and the Caribbean, the model country of the north became the *bully with the stick*, the imperialistic exploiter, the main enemy of leftist revolutionaries, who seek to use the ideal of cultural unity to achieve political solidarity. This goal can be seen in the quotation used previously regarding language, partially repeated below. Note the call to cultural unity as a "starting point," also the reference to "imperial violence."

> Let us intensify the consciousness of cultural unity, and from it we will attain the remaining unities. Contemporary history has demonstrated fully that imperial violence cannot sever with the sword what the Word has joined.[20]

---

[18] Arróm, p. 215.

[19] Arróm, p. 216.

[20] Luis Brito García, p. 115.

The allusion seems clear. For the author of the quotation imperial violence comes from the United States. For others this country may have another meaning. Be this as it may, now that the United States has become the exporter of technology and popular culture—providing asylum for millions of Hispanic refugees, who through communication media (such as Univisión) have begun to export their experience in the *monster* (the U.S. in a reference made by José Martí)—obviously, any search for cultural identity has to take into account its omnipresence.[21]

The degree to which the influence of the United States on Latin America is perceived varies, of course, from those who are unaware of its presence—the Mexican *comisario,* whose comments were cited in the previous chapter—to the middle class Marxist-Leninist revolutionaries who write diatribe denouncing the cultural imperialism of the United States while wearing *blue jeans* and listening to *rock* music. Carlos Alberto Montaner writes a similar example regarding communists, who supposedly resent the *imperialistic influence.* He summarizes it by saying that "Even anti-Americanism is a typically American product."[22] Possibly they wear *blue jeans* without realizing it, the same way that the *comisario* of 50 years ago may still not have a precise idea of the United States as a distinct entity among "those countries out there." Maybe he does not even know exactly where his grandchildren go on their pilgrimage in order to return with dollars, or the source of the strident music that they prefer over the traditional *boleros* and *rancheras.* In one way or another, with variable degrees of perception, most Hispanic Americans are resigned to the influence of that other culture in the New World. They reveal varying degrees of admiration and resentment towards the Colossus of the North. Perhaps they are less worried about the contradictions of their attitude than the Mexican business man, who would say in the way of a prologue, that he was not a *malinchista,* that is, a person who sells out to the foreigner like Malinche, Hernán Cortés' *mistress* and collaborator in the conquest of Mexico.[23]

---

[21] Carlos Alberto Montaner, *200 Years of Gringos* (Translated by Gastón Fernández de la Torriente and James F. Horton, Univ. Press of America: Lanham-New York-London, 1983), p. vii.

[22] op. cit., p. 4.

[23] A university professor of literature, Salvador Velasco, correctly made me notice that this phrase reveals a modern prejudice. His question was the following: "In the 16th Century, to whom did Malintzin owe loyalty, since

The Colossal Geography of the Americas: New Worldism

Long before the influence of the United States would incite Latin Americans, especially Hispanic Americans, to define their cultural identity in a negative way, as opposed to that of Anglo-Saxon America, the colossal geography of all the Americas became a literary theme from the time of the Conquest, and the topic of countless *sobremesas* (prolonged after dinner conversations) to this day. Nature, real and imagined, became not only a literary theme, but soon began to differentiate the inhabitants of the New World from those of the Old.

> Those Spaniards who came from a literature in which nature barely appears, immediately and by necessity, are going to write the most prolific and loving descriptions of the natural world that Europe had known until then.[24]

At first the New World's utopian and abundant promise, though barbarous, was contrasted with the known and meager one of the Old World. Initially Anglo-Saxon America also was included in this promise, which contrasted the two Worlds, but as the promise, with later and less prosperous beginnings, has been fulfilled in North America, it has eluded the hopes of many Hispanic nations, as well as parts of Brazil. Therefore, today's Latin American New Worldism is mixed with the negative cultural definition (discussed earlier), that of a Latin America opposed to Anglo-Saxon America.

Furthermore, besides the considerations that come from geographical difficulties, Latin Americans have tried to explain their lack of progress in comparison with the United States, and their dependence on this country, first by discounting the importance of material progress while proclaiming their cultural superiority—an interpretation coming from Enrique Rodo's *Ariel*—and afterwards by exonerating themselves from blame for their backwardness. By means of a Marxist economic analysis, they blame the United States and other

---

the Mexican nation, such as it is today, did not exist?" Moreover, he stressed the importance of Doña Marina's role, that of a "truly extraordinary woman," in the conquest of Mexico.

[24] Arturo Uslar Pietri, "Lo criollo en la literatura," in *Las nubes* (Prólogo de Mariano Picón Salas, Santiago de Chile: Editorial Universitaria, 1956), p. 67.

industrialized countries calling them exploiters. This attitude is combined with the ambivalent perception of cultural differences that paint the North Americans as coarse and materialistic, with the result that many Latin American prefer their own customs, although they may admire U.S. material superiority. Nowadays many are troubled by the suspicion that this superiority may be more than material. Has not *Calibán*, the figure in *Ariel* taken to symbolize the United States, constructed better libraries and universities?[25] Nevertheless, many aristocratically minded Latin Americans consider the manners of the North American individual to be coarse. How can he, or she, have taken higher-level university courses than they have—frequently the case—and still put their dirty bare feet up on the furniture? The explanation lies in that *ser educado* (to be well brought up), is much more than *to be educated,* a phrase that is confused with only having gone to a college or university. In any event, the cultural solidarity of the Latin American nations, despite their ideology, political posture, right, left, or type of government, dictatorship or democracy, became clear when they sided with Argentina against England, the mother country of the United States, in the war over the Malvinas, or Falkland Islands. This cultural identification occurred in spite of the fact that from a political point of view, several Latin American countries had condemned the military government of Argentina for its *dirty war* against any opposition. And the Latin Americans' sense of identity reached a feverish pitch when the United States took England's side, uniting them in their New Worldism, opposed to both the Old World and the Anglo-Saxon exploiters.

One can gather from the above that the New World's promise of marvels, in which its universal geography plays a prominent role, now has become a problem, while at the same time it is a source of pride, and one of the reasons for Latin America's well known regionalism, which is paraded with the names of flora and fauna together with the names and characteristics of relatives and friends in unending after dinner conversations. First, the following quotation illustrates the idea of geography as a problem:

> The historic view of Latin America is that it is a thrill. Huge mountains, lush jungles, exotic wealth and poverty, bloody politics–this is the exciting continent. The image has obsessed not only tourists and artists but also

---

[25] Montaner, p. ix.

businessmen, churchmen and statesmen, and revolutionaries. Its strongest enthusiasts now are the New Leftists . . . There is a darker view of Latin America, that it is a bore. Incredibly various, dense and complicated, resentful of change, in constant pain, it is the depressing continent.[26]

Whether the image they have of their land is optimistic or somber, Latin Americans see it as their own. They are frequently heard using the possessive *our,* when referring to their land or their countries. They use phrases like "Our customs are like that," or "In our countries this or that happens." Phrases like this establish a common link, and show their intimate relationship with the land, which, unlike that of the United States, does not let itself be tamed.

The view of the land as a barbaric and indomitable force first appeared in the well-known book, *Facundo: civilización y barbarie.* In it Domingo Faustino Sarmiento portrays man of that time imbued with a wild nature, opposed to civilization, which will come with the transplant of Europeans, and by following the educational model of the United States. Despite a massive immigration to Argentina, Uruguay, and southern Brazil at the end of the 19th century and beginning of the 20th, Sarmiento's civilizing model has been only partly fulfilled. In general, what has predominated in Latin America, both in literature and after dinner conversations, is the image of a disproportionate nature, which at the same can discourage, because of its overwhelming force, and enthuse because of its abundance. Nature seems to dominate man, not the reverse, as in the United States, and as soon as one manages to take advantage of the abundance there is, others take it away, the United States and the international enterprises, with the help of the resident oligarchy. Latin Americans, who consider that they are the legitimate heirs of the abundance, of the promise announced by the chroniclers, feel powerless and cheated. They see themselves grafted onto their world, onto a babaric, but prolific land, sacked by others, of which they are able to take advantage if they too collaborate, or, if on the contrary, they resist and shake off the "yoke of American imperialism." All want to consider themselves "legitimate heirs," even the collaborating oligarchs, whose anti-American rhetoric at times is

---

[26] "Priest of Revolution: Camilo Torres," *The New York Review of Books,* Oct. 23, 1969, Vol. 13, No. 7, p. 13. Transcribed above is the original text in English, cited and translated into Spanish by Robert G. Meade, Jr., in "Imágenes y realidades interamericanas," *Cuadernos Americanos,* Nov.-Dec., 1973, p. 36.

barely distinguishable from that of the rebels who seek to implant their own socialist system, which supposedly will avoid the errors of the countries that have abandoned it. Now most Latin American intellectuals, just as Octavio Paz did years ago, must admit that socialism is an import that does not take root, the same as the *democracy* imported from the United States. Of course, the great majority of Latin Americans are not rich oligarchs or rebels. Nevertheless, whatever their political orientation may be, often tinged with nationalistic rhetoric, they seek to enjoy, the same as the *noble conquistadores,* the abundance of their disproportionate geography, which has helped forge their cultural heritage, affecting their politics, their economy, their literature, and their art.

As we shall see when speaking later of the Colonial unity, this geography is constituted in part by the genes, the labor and the products of the Indians.[27] In politics geography has contributed to the continuation of authoritarian and personalistic governments, states that perpetuate attitudes in their citizens that are both hopeful and skeptical. In the economy it has reinforced the predominance of regional interests, devoted mainly to the exploitation and export of primary resources to collect foreign exchange for the importation of luxury items, and to continue taking advantage of cheap and abundant labor. In literature, contact with the new lands gave rise to a baroque abundance and complication of elaborate forms.[28] And in art the disproportionate geography of the Americas has had influence in creating a multitude of primitive and dynamic forms as a result of Iberian civilization grafted onto the indigenous population, above all in Mexico, Guatemala, and the Andean countries. Also, in some places there are art forms to which black African features are added.[29] If one accepts the premise that the indigenous people found by the Spaniards and Portuguese are an integral part of the Americas, one can include under the title of this section the fact that an essential characteristic of Latin Americans is due to the influence of another race and culture. This is true even in Argentina and Uruguay, which were *mestizo* countries until the beginning of the 20th century. The adjectives *disproportionate* and *colossal* can be used with impunity to describe the marvels of the cities

---

[27] Uslar Pietri, "La geografía del trabajo," *Las nubes*, p. 32.

[28] Uslar Pietri, "Lo criollo en la literatura," *Las nubes*, p. 72.

[29] Uslar Pietri, "Out of the Tropics: An Avant-Garde Art," *UNESCO Courier*, Aug.-Sept., 1977, p. 32.

of Tenochtitlán and Cuzco, which so amazed Hernán Cortés and Francisco Pizarro.

To bring this section to a close while providing a summary and comment, several implications suggested by what was said above about the influence of Latin America's geography on its inhabitants should be pointed out. Geography has played a greater role than in the U.S., whether as a marvel, promise, or barbarous and indomitable force, in short, as a problem. Part of this problem lies in the objective, measurable, and scientific fact that the Latin American continent has more barriers in the form of distances, mountain ranges, jungles, and deserts, without including the indigenous population, whose descendants—in different stages of westernization—continue to be part of the geography. For example, lands, distances, and the continuing presence of peasants dedicated to subsistence agriculture, make economic development difficult. Another part of this problem stems from the attitudes that the land has fostered in the Latin American character, attitudes that are subjective, full of complexes, and paradoxical. These are the ones we want to note below.

City and country evidence show profound differences, which point to oppositions between civilization and barbarism, Europeans and Indians, city dwellers and peasants, literate and illiterate, the incorporated and the marginalized, the developed and the backward, colonizers and colonized. We can extend these schematic oppositions to a land at man's service, or domesticated, versus an indomitable and barbarous land. In Latin America its barbarous elements and the pessimistic attitude resulting from having failed in trying to tame it, impregnate the psychological atmosphere of the urbanites. On the other hand, one could say that in a schematic way that in the United States the opposite occurs: civilization from the city irradiates toward the country, domesticating and controlling it. This control is rooted in optimism fed by a long series of economic and technological successes. By comparison many Latin Americans, more in the Hispanic countries than in Brazil, cannot overcome their pessimism when they feel that they are members of the world's periphery. They feel marginalized, dominated, and exploited by the center, the metropolis, that is, the industrialized countries, as if they were part of the *country*, relegated only to provide raw materials for the benefit of the industrial machine and the citizenry of the United States and Europe, plus the resident oligarchs. The oligarchs, like the Colonial masters, the same as migrating birds, even after centuries, when seeing themselves threatened—if the counterinsurgency force at their disposal does not work—take flight and go to Miami, Chicago, San Francisco, Paris, or Madrid. They *return* to the metropolis with their possessions. Later we will see that this summary is not so simple, but let it suffice for the moment.

In light of the foregoing comment that Latin Americans feel a more intimate attachment to their land than North Americans, now it seems paradoxical that they should leave it. The paradox can be explained by saying that the love they have for their land does not necessarily entail optimism regarding their political and economic security. Latin Americans may love their land—everything related to memories, music, relatives, friends, food, trees and fruits—and at the same time see the possibility of a better future for their country with the skepticism and shrewdness born of disappointment. They distrust the ability of their government employees, or officers, and the official versions of what they do. Their experience with an unstable and violent past, and a present without the perspective of overcoming, makes them distrust everything not saved by relatives, friends, the *compadre,* the *padrino* (co-godfather and godfather), or the rhetoric of the moment. Their relationship with the land is included in this context. On the one hand, in prolonged *sobremesas* (after dinner conversations), they describe and praise its fruits in abundant detail, but on the other they are disappointed to see their land still exploited by a resident minority and by foreigners, further that its disproportion and barbarity are mixed with human disproportion and barbarity.

When comparing the optimistic attitude of North Americans in being able to control nature for their benefit with the pessimistic attitude of Hispanic Americans—if not Brazilians—we can conjecture that feeling dominated by nature is due in part to the speed and scope of the Conquest. It left the Spaniards and their descendants, both *criollos* (initially descendants of Spaniards) and *mestizos* (people of mixed blood), grafted onto another civilization. This contrasts sharply with the limited, slow and gradual expansion of the North American colonies, established as a transplant—and not a graft—in territory domesticated by killing or removing the Indians.[30]

We must note in passing that the Portuguese also did not complete their conquest of Brazil immediately and quickly like the Spaniards. That is why today Brazilians seem to feel less overwhelmed by the

---

[30] Uslar Pietri, "La geografía del trabajo," *Las nubes*, p. 32.

nature of their country. The Portuguese did not immediately go into the continent like the Spaniards. During half a century they limited their actions to establishing small economic bases at several strategic points on the coast to export first brazilwood, and later sugar cane syrup. The conquest was carried out much later, as in the United States, although the economy based on slavery, similar in some aspects to that of the U.S. South, is profoundly different to that of the North, where neither slavery or racial mixing took root. We should add that this model is the one that predominated in the United States, aside from the fact that little white and black racial mixing occurred in the South. On the contrary, in Brazil, as in Hispanic America, much racial mixing has occurred with the consequent problems of integration, but we repeat, the Brazilians, despite the geography of their country, in some respects as colossal as that of the Hispanic Americans, have a less pessimistic attitude towards it. Perhaps it is this way, because it was just a short time ago that they started to populate the *interior,* a synonym for *savage.* Perhaps now some of them are discouraged with the ecological disasters brought about in the Amazon, and that as for populating the interior, my colleague's ironic prediction that Brazil is not the country of the future is right. This may be true with regard to certain areas of the country, but others are very developed, for example the State of São Paulo. In Brazil there are contrasts as sharp as in Hispanic America when comparing the city with the countryside, or the coast, and the south with the interior. One also ought to recognize that as regards feeling overwhelmed by savage nature, the *retirantes* (refugees from drought) in the *Nordeste* (Brazil's Northeast) may not have a positive attitude toward nature. However, they are not the majority, and if what they have is not optimism, it is stubbornness, because they plant again in the areas where they know that sometimes it does not rain for years, but where they also may face terrible floods.

Finally it is fitting to point out under the title of Latin America's *colossal geography* the problem of conscience, or the identity crisis of many Latin American intellectuals. It emerges from the oppositions, or dichotomies noted earlier: city/country, civilization/barbarity, center/periphery, or in other words, Europe and the United States versus Latin America. Due to their historical cultural heritage from the European side and to personal circumstances of family and education, they are city dwellers—civilized—cosmopolitan heirs of the universal values of Western civilization, above all those of its art and letters. They also appreciate the aristocratic refinement that comes to them from Europe. But they want to be Americans (in the sense of belonging to the New World). How should they relate to their land? Besides, they want to participate in the benefits of the comfort and technology that emanate from the industrialized countries, especially the United States, the new center. As descendants of Iberian ancestors from the Catholic center of civilization, for some time now they have seen themselves displaced to the periphery. They have searched unsuccessfully in other countries, and in ideologies imported from the metropolis that replaces Spain and Portugal. Now more than ever they have to face the dilemma of reconciling their Western heritage with their peripheral and dependent situation, as *mestizos* of the New World. Faced with the many problems of their countries, they have to choose an authentic path for themselves.

The Colonial Unity

Of course the common cultural characteristics treated below have been unfolding in one way or another as a result of the *Colonial Unity.* In politics, the monopolistic Colonial administration—first under the hegemony of the Catholics Monarchs, Ferdinand and Isabella, followed by the Hapsburgs and the Bourbons, which during the reign of Phillip II included Portugal—produced the stability that allowed the Spaniards and the Portuguese to impose their language and Catholicism, while at the same they mixed their genes with those of a considerable percentage of the indigenous population. This process was not completed, but its extent is amazing when one takes into account the immensity of the Iberian Empire. One cannot deny that as a result of the process just mentioned, Colonial society was left with a hierarchy. First came those born in Spain or Portugal (inhabitants of the Iberian Peninsula); then the *criollos,* at first descendants of a peninsular father and mother, or a peninsular father; afterwards the *mestizos,* children of a peninsular father and Indian concubine, or of other *mestizos.* Next to last came the Indians, and finally the African slaves. However, all elements of society, excepting (at first) African slaves, were incorporated by the Church. For example, the Indians, despite their fate in other ways—being obligated to work for landowners and miners—felt that they were part of an order, although theirs was the last rung (or the penultimate, where there were blacks). According to Octavio Paz, feeling that they were incorporated as Christians filled the void that they felt when they saw the gods of their temples destroyed.

This possibility of belonging to a living order, even if it was at the bottom of the social pyramid, was cruelly denied to the Indians by the Protestants of New England. It is often forgotten that to belong to the Catholic faith meant that one found a place in the cosmos. The flight of their gods and the death of their leaders had left the natives in a solitude so complete that it is difficult for a modern man to imagine it. Catholicism re-established their ties with the world and the other world. It gave them back a sense of their place on earth; it nurtured their hopes and justified their lives and deaths.[31]

By giving the Indians a place in the "world," as well as in the "other world," the Church contributed to Colonial stability and stratification, making the yoke of their labor less intolerable. Their lot became worse after Independence—in some countries towards the end of the 19th century under liberal governments—when the Colonial statutes protecting their lands were revoked. For example, in Mexico, under the liberal regime of Benito Juárez and the dictatorship of Porfirio Díaz they lost many of their communal lands. They were adversely affected, because they were unable, as before, to exercise their preference to live apart from the main population stream by having recourse to these statutes. On the other hand, blacks, *mestizos,* and *mulatos,* who made up a large part of the lower social strata of the cities, took advantage of Independence, because, unlike the Indians, they participated actively and willingly in it, which already indicated a process of integration, driven by ever more widespread *mestizaje* (miscegenation). But one must not forget that this process was made possible in the first place by the inclusion of Indians (and later of blacks) in the Colonial hierarchical society.[32] It has continued until now, to the extent that most Latin Americans today, besides being nominally Catholic and speaking Spanish or Portuguese, have a mixed cultural heritage.

Mestizaje, Syncretism, Abundance, Baroque

If one were obligated to speak of Latin America in terms of a single cultural feature, the one that stands out most is *mestizaje*—mixing, in variable degrees, races and cultures of the Old World with the New.

---

[31] Octavio Paz, *The Labyrinth of Solitude* (New York: Grove Press, Inc., 1961), p. 102.

[32] Tim Guldimann, *Lateinamerika: Die Entwicklung der Unterentwicklung* (Munich: Verlag C. H. Beck, 1975), p. 39.

Arturo Uslar Pietri stresses the importance of *mestizaje* as a deeply Hispanic American characteristic, emphasizing the difference between a "transplant" and a "graft."

> Hispanic American life, in what it has as most characteristic and profound, is conditioned not by a transplant, but by a graft . . . .. That process of accommodation, approximation, and even fusion of what is foreign and its opposite, which has gone on now during four long centuries, is the [process] that produces what is peculiarly Hispanic American, which is neither Spanish nor Indian, both modified irreparably through mutual contact, but rather something else, which from the start was to be called *criollo*, whose essential feature was *mestizaje*. Sometimes physical *mestizaje*, but always spiritual.[33]

The presence of *mestizaje*, at least "spiritual," is still felt in many parts of so-called white countries, such as Argentina. The word "graft" in the above quotation refers to Hispanic America, to the fact that the first two viceroyalties of the Spanish Empire were established and built on the foundations of two indigenous empires, those of the Aztecs and the Incas, and they developed in accord with the availability of Indian labor.

> More than geographical relief, more than the original direction of the colonizing stream, the distribution of indigenous labor is what determines during almost all of the colonial period, the shapes, the development and the location of the Spanish Empire.[34]

Perhaps the image of a "graft" cannot be applied as conveniently to Brazil and the coasts of the Hispanic American countries of the Caribbean, where, since there were fewer Indians available to work, the mixing of whites with blacks brought from Africa prevailed.

In Latin America nothing is pure, whether we speak of races, architecture, literature (excepting some Colonial poetry), or religion. As for the latter, priests let the Indians preserve some of their beliefs and customs in the Catholic ritual. This syncretism continues until now. The common experience of most Latin Americans in the first years of

---

[33] Uslar Pietri, "La geografía del trabajo," *Las nubes*, p. 32. (The translation of this quotation from Spanish is mine, as well as others from this author.)

[34] p. 32.

the Colonial period was contact with the Indians, and a colossal nature offering a tremendous variety of plants and animals. The abundance cited by Arturo Uslar Pietri in an essay called "Lo criollo en la literatura" could be a factor that influences what this writer describes as follows:

[The] Hispanic American taste for the most elaborate and difficult forms, for the most cultured and artistic forms of expression, [which] not only is manifested in their literature and their art, but is reflected in everyday life and in popular art.

The profusion of nature in the New World also is a factor that contributes to the "long permanence of the baroque and the profound identification of the *criollo* soul with this style."[35]

The following list is an example of only some of the products that would not let the European who had come to the Americas be the same as before:

. . cacao (from which cocoa and chocolate are made), maize (Indian corn), the potato and sweet potato, the yuca or manioc, the tomato, the avocado, the peanut, the guava, the papaya, the pineapple, the sapota and the sapotilla (which, besides being luscious fruit, also produce the chicle from which chewing gum is made), the trees from which rubber is extracted, tobacco, cacti, American agave or aloe (from which fiber for rope is made), yerba maté or maté (from which a drink is made by infusion), the quina or cinchona tree (from which quinine is extracted), ipecacuana (a medicinal root), jalapa (another medicinal plant), the guayacan or lignum vitae tree, sarsaparilla, coca, vanilla, logwood (*palo de campeche,* used for dyes), brazilwood, mahogany, jacaranda or palisander, and species of bean, gourds, red peppers, palms, pines and cotton plants.[36]

Part of the mixture, or of *mestizaje,* although it may not be biological, is the contact itself with the new continent. I cannot imagine life without the majority of these products, and although I do not remember having eaten all the fruits, for example the *zapote* (the Spanish word for *sapota* in the above quotation), I use, or frequently hear the expression that somebody fell like a *zapote,* or in Spanish that

---

[35] *Las nubes*, p. 72.

[36] Pedro Henríquez Hureña, *A Concise History of Latin American Culture,* (New York: Frederick A. Praeger, Inc., 1966), p. 10.

"fulano cayó como zapote," or that he fell flat on his face, he let himself be deceived, or taken in.

Arturo Uslar Pietri points out that very soon differences began to appear between the Spaniards called *indianos* (those who had come to the Indies, or the Americas) and those of the Old World, likewise between *criollos* (Spaniards born in the Americas) and peninsular Spaniards, without mentioning the mixed heritage of the *mestizos,* who were not freely accepted in the Hispanic society of their fathers, nor in the indigenous society of their mothers, who thus had to rely on their wits to make a way for themselves. More will be said of the *mestizos* later. Now, as for differences between *criollos* and peninsular Spaniards, the latter thought that the former developed early, mentally and physically, and that they were witty in their conversation. However, while still young they would start to show signs of senility. On the other hand, the *criollos* considered the peninsular Spaniards to be rude and lacking in grace and wit.[37]

Personalism and Verbalism

Now we can deal with two cultural features that are derived from the Colonial experience, and *mestizaje,* an integral part of the former in all of Latin America. One must not forget that the massive migration to Argentina, Uruguay, and southern Brazil does not occur until close to the end of the 19th century. *Personalism*, in the sense of the high esteem placed on the individual daring and bravery of a warrior chieftain, goes back to the Early Middle Ages. Appreciation of the individual worth has been pointed out as a cultural characteristic of the Visigoths, who before the Moorish invasion and occupation, had already been romanized and Christianized. Then the warrior-like experiences throughout the long centuries of the Reconquest, aside from those in the New World, heightened the importance of the strong individual and his ability to remedy *sui generis* the problems faced by his followers, friends, and relatives.

Evidence of Hispanic American *personalism* is abundant, and this cultural feature is not lacking in Brazil.[38] The importance of the *person*

---

[37] Op. cit., p. 66.

[38] Personalism is one of the many *isms* cited by Julius Rivera in *Latin America: a sociocultural interpretation* (enlarged edition, New York: Irvington Publishers, 1978), pp. 131-132.

is evident in the phrase *"dignidad de la persona"* (dignity of the person), which Spanish essayists cite as a democratic counterbalance to rigid social hierarchies. The many *caudillos* that have marched across the Latin American stage—from Santa Anna to Fidel Castro—are examples of personalistic and charismatic leaders. Throughout the unstable history of Hispanic America—and to a certain degree the same can be said about Brazil—people have trusted individuals rather than impersonal systems, although much lip service has been given to the letter of the law and the many constitutions so often violated.[39]

The custom of seeking out a person to remedy a problem in times of trouble, a relative, friend, or *compadre* (co-godfather), preferably the *patrón* (the boss, master, employer), is reflected in the popular saying, *"el que a buen árbol se arrima, buena sombra lo cobija* (he who stands under a good tree is protected by good shade)." Solutions to problems are found through persons. When Pedro Páramo learns from his administrator that he has debts from his inheritance of the Media Luna, his response is personalistic, not quantitative: *"¿A quién le debemos? No me importa cuánto sino a quién.* (Who do we owe? I don't care how much, but who)."[40] The network of personal relations, relatives and friends, whose attributes and actions parade through the conversation of the *sobremesa* testify to the Latin American's reliance on people rather than things. A complementary aspect of this preference is localism, loyalty to the *patria chica* (one's home *country*, or region).[41]

---

[39] "I have never heard people talk so much about constitutions—says Andre Siegfried—as in those countries where the Constitution is violated everyday. Eminent jurists discuss seriously and conscientiously the meaning of the texts that the polititians mock, and if one smiles, the doctors in jurisprudence point with their finger to the articles that are the guarantee of the law. The law has majesty only in words." Samuel Ramos, *El perfil del hombre y de la cultura en México* (México: Imprenta Mundial, 1934), p. 53. (The translation from Spanish is mine.)

[40] Juan Rulfo, *Pedro Páramo* (Edited by Luis Leal, New York: Appleton-Century Crofts, 1970), p. 47.

[41] There are many, and varied references to Spanish and Hispanic American regionalism. Examples are the regionalism indicated by Frank Tannenbaum as one of the "keys" to Latin America in his *Ten Keys to Latin America* (New York: Vintage Books, 1966), pp. 66-76, and the following statement by Julius Rivera (pp. 129-30): "Regionalism buttressed by geographical isolation has been one of the most burdensome handicaps in the progress of Latin America."

Américo Castro points to the motives of this complementary relation, or the mutual support between personalism and localism, in the Spanish context, as follows:

> The person does not come out of himself, and aspires to attract to himself everything that exists around him. The only social life in which he truly believes and in which he participates, is founded on emotional coincidences that lack a fund of ideas or depersonalized tasks. Hence the associations whose central link is a caudillo, the local political boss, or a common messianic hope.[42]

This quotation applies also to Latin America, where there are caudillos and political bosses, besides many examples of messianic hope, founded on a new president, on Fidel Castro, Che Guevara, or on a religious fanatic like Antonio Conselheiro.[43]

There is no doubt that personalism is a cultural trait inherited from Spain, let us say the Iberian Peninsula, and it need not come only from the Visigoths, who only provide an example of its long history. Miguel de Unamuno's repeated insistence on the *"hombre de carne y hueso"* (literally man of flesh and bone) must be the primary source of the following quotation:

> Individualism or personalism is the key to Spain's genius. Man is the very center of the Spaniard's universe: not a mere philosophical concept of man or of humanity as an abstraction, but a man of flesh and bone, of loves and hatreds.[44]

---

[42] *La realidad histórica de España* (5a. ed., México: Editorial Porrúa, 1973), p. 261. (The translation of this quotation from Spanish is mine, as well as others from the same author. In the "person," reference is made to both men and women.)

[43] Antonio Conselheiro led a rebellion against the republican government of Brazil at the end of the 19th Century, which was put down in the Canudos Campaign, the subject Euclides da Cunha's master work, *Os Sertões (Campanha de Canudos)*, published for the first time in Rio de Janeiro by Laemmert y Cía. in December, 1902. The first historical episode is the main subject matter of a novel by Mario Vargas Llosa called *La guerra del fin del mundo* (Barcelona: Seix Barral, 1981).

[44] Robert J. Havighurst et al., in *La sociedad y educación en América Latina* (Buenos Aires, 1962), p. 39.

Américo Castro confirms the Latin American inheritance of Iberian personalism, as follows: "For the Iberoamerican, persons have an absolute value, and exist by following an orbit that begins and ends in themselves." With this statement as a premise, the Spanish essayist elaborates, stressing the consequences of giving more value to persons than to things:

> Their culture is very rich in everything that can be done without conversing [or dealing] with things: bravery, heroism, personal dignity, richness of inner life expressed with beauty, distinction or grace, religiosity, poetry, all forms of popular art (textiles, ceramics, songs, dances). In a word, everything that can be done without coming out of oneself. Rather than individualistic, such a way of life should be called personalistic and integral. Persons, we repeat, have an absolute value; work to modify things around them is not a prime function in the life of the Iberoamerican.[45]

Now I can make some observations, both personal and bibliographic, over the other cultural trait of this section. *Verbalism* is the complement of *personalism*. Just as *personalism*, it can be considered an Iberian heritage. The following quotation, which refers to the Spaniard, is also applicable to the Portuguese, although in the latter it may be a less outstanding characteristic.

> He likes to converse and show his ingenuity in conversation. No people are more loquacious, nor do they express themselves with greater fluency and intensity. It is difficult to imagine a taciturn Spaniard, or one that has trouble finding the right word. This gift of speech was transmitted to the New World with all of its force, and in some places it has adopted the flowery exuberance of the topics.[46]

Angel Rosenblat, among other writers, points to the loquacity of the Spaniard, and suggests in the quotation cited here that it is a substitute for action (perhaps the warrior-like action of the Reconquest, terminated in 1492), and characteristic of all social classes:

---

[45] *Iberoamérica* (3a. ed., New York: Holt, Rinehart and Winston, 1963), pp. 253-54. (The translation of this quotation from Spanish is mine, as well as others from this author. It should be noted that use of the masculine pronoun does not exclude women.)

[46] Havighurst, p. 60. (The translation from Spanish is mine.)

And when the impetus of external action was spent, or lost, reverence of the word remained, the elegance of the word. In the Castilian countryside the traveler finds beggars who speak like true gentlemen, with grace and dignity. The word became a sign of national genius.[47]

Rhetorical skill was also cultivated assiduously in the colonies. According to Uslar Pietri, a Venezuelan writer cited several times earlier, the *indiano* and the *criollo* developed their verbal skill in order to compensate for their disadvantageous position vis-à-vis the peninsular Spaniard. In the following quotation Uslar Pietri alludes to Lope de Vegas' characterization of the *indiano's* speech:

> How the affectation of his language makes them laugh. On hearing someone speak using over-elaborated arguments and rare words, one begins to think that he is an *indiano*. There is something like a preference for the contrived expression that runs parallel to the ostentation of his garments and his riches. That learned, affected, and prolific language distinguished him from those who heard him on the Peninsula.[48]

In general it seems to me that in Latin America one converses more than in the United States. People love to converse to entertain themselves. One hears extremely long stories at the *sobremesa* (sitting around the table after a meal). The same story is told in more and more detail. Long and ceremonious speeches are normal, required to observe protocol in situations thought to demand it. Thank you speeches should be long and effusive. Reciprocal praise found in the prologue of many books, and expressed in the most ingenious language possible, is further evidence of *verbalism*.

The quick answer, sharp and ingenious, is highly valued, as exemplified in the verses of the *payadores* (singers who perform improvised musical dialogue), in the banter heard on the soccer field, or between spectators at the bullfight in the *sol* section (the one exposed to the sun), and in the comments with double meaning exchanged during the *sobremesa*.

---

[47] Angel Rosenblat, *La primera visión de América y otros estudios* (2a ed., Caracas: Ministerio de Educación, Dirección Técnica, Depto. de Publicaciones, 1969), p. 52. (The translation of this quotation is mine, as well as others from this author.)

[48] "Aquellos indianos," *Las nubes*, p. 55.

Defeating an opponent verbally brings praise to the winner and humiliation to the loser. Many years ago I witnessed a very brief, but decisive verbal duel on a college campus in Eastern Oregon. It took place between two Latin Americans, a Peruvian and a Costa Rican, who together with two others had started to play soccer to remind themselves of home. I do not remember exactly, but the Peruvian was doing something to the Costa Rican that he did not like. Maybe he had been kicking him or scoring goals against some rule. The Costa Rican, who was known to be unable to hold his temper, became furious, and warned the other in a low, grave voice, as if it were an ultimatum: "If you do that to me again I'll bust your face (*Si me volvés a hacer eso te rompo la cara.*)." The Peruvian's immediate reply was: "And I'll stick my foot in your nose (*Y yo te pongo la pata en la nariz.*)." Said in a light tone, almost in a falsetto, to make fun of the Costa Rican's terrifying tone, in the context of the soccer game, the Peruvian's witty retort implying that he would also bust the furious Costa Rican's face with a kick, similar to the successful ones that perhaps had motivated the ultimatum, won for him everyone's laughter and the verbal victory, besides the game. The Costa Rican went off totally humiliated and did not reappear until the next day. A Guatemalan friend of mine, experienced in the double-entendre and word play of Mexico would spend his time instructing me about the importance of the quick reply. For a long time he kept reminding me that I should emulate the Peruvian's example.

Latin Americans seem to be ready at any moment to express an opinion, expound on a subject about which they may have no objective or statistically based information. People have a higher regard for the eloquence with which an argument is expressed than for any factual base. What is important is who states an opinion, and how convincingly it is expressed. The following comment illustrates the close link between *personalism* and *verbalism,* and, moreover, points to the Latin American's need to talk convincingly, regardless of factual support:

> A man has to speak as often as possible, even to himself if he does not have an audience, and when he speaks to himself he does so as to an audience. His speech is not merely a communication of ideas; it is giving of a part of himself because a man's ideas are himself. Thus, for the Latin American, speaking is not just an exchange, but an attempt to convince, to proselytize and also not to be convinced. . . Ideas and emotions are not separated.[49]

---

[49] Rivera, p. 2.

Ortega y Gasset's comment on the psychology of the *pronunciamientos* (manifestos) in Spain—which also can be applied to Latin America—illustrates the link between *verbalism* and the personalistic, charismatic *caudillo,* whose power rests largely on his rhetorical skill.[50] One of the negative implications of *verbalism* is its connection with demagoguery, with *caudillismo* (the *caudillo's* system of government). The convincing rhetoric and personality of the strong, charismatic, and clever *caudillo* draw people along. The success of Fidel Castro is one of the clearest examples of *personalism* and *verbalism.* People follow him because of his personal magnetism, part of which is due to his well-known rhetorical skill.

The experience of the Colonial period and the civil strife of the 19th and 20th centuries have made Hispanic Americans, particularly the *mestizos,* distrustful of systems or institutions. It has made them rely on personal relationships and on their own ingenuity and keenness. Thus they compensate for the lack of real power with rhetoric. Development of rhetorical skill has been important in Hispanic America as a means to gain power, to compensate for an inferiority complex, to outdo those of the class or group one wishes to emulate. The *conquistadors* want to outdo the *hidalgos* of Spain; the *criollos* the peninsular Spaniards; the *mestizos* the *criollos;* the Indians the *mestizos.* This emulation has been taking place since the *hidalguización* (ennobling) of the *conquistadores,* immediately following the Conquest. [51]

North Americans in general tend to express fewer opinions, support their arguments with facts, or remain silent. In comparison with Latin Americans they seem taciturn, or at least less verbally effusive. Although it may appear to be a rash generalization, overall, North Americans seem less predisposed to developing their rhetoric, and even

---

[50] "Sure that almost all the world was of their opinion, though perhaps in secret, they had a blind faith in the magic effect of 'pronouncing' a phrase." *Invertebrate Spain* (Translation and Foreword by Mildred Adams, New York: Howard Fertig, 1974), p. 54.

[51] In this regard one should remember Charles Wagley's discussion in Chapter 2 from *The Latin American Tradition* (New York: Columbia University Press, 1968), also the comments of Vernon Fluharty regarding the relations of the "middle group" with the aristocracy in "The Colombian Upper Class," from *Dance of the Millions* (Pittsburgh: Univ. of Pittsburgh Press, 1957). The reference to "hidalguización" is from Angel Rosenblat, op. cit., p. 57.

seem less skilled verbally, partly because they do not practice the art of everyday conversation as much as Latin Americans. Hispanic Americans—and Brazilians also, from what I have seen in Brazil—are more talkative, and consequently more skilled in their rhetoric. A Mexican psychologist, Rogelio Díaz Guerrero, points to the Mexican's need to talk constantly, because he/she assumes that interpersonal reality can be modified at will.[52] Talking is part of this modification, and is needed for self-actualization and esteem. Unsatisfied need explains why the Mexican must talk incessantly with friends.[53]

On the other hand, Américo Castro affirms once again the link between *personalism* and *verbalism,* and at the same time suggests one of the motives for the North American's reticence to express opinions:

> In general one can say that intellectual superiority (speaking, writing, and thinking with some distinction) creates a consciousness of refinement; a North American will consider the expression of feeling himself different, and the use of it to underscore distance and superiority with regard to his neighbor, as a manifestation of arrogance and a lack of human charity . . . They do not understand that the American shrinks inwardly when the moment comes to say "I," and to express opinions and judgements that make him feel personally important as an isolated individual and not as a member of his country or of any collective institution.[54]

Another connection between the two cultural traits under discussion can be illustrated through contrasting the Latin American's attitude toward work with that of the Anglo-Saxon, or Protestant:

> Whatever its origin may be—or its origins—resistance against the heavy yoke of work seems inherent to Hispanic individualism (Américo Castro

---

[52] He stresses this necessity by describing what he and so many others have observed: "This incessant talking seems to be a profound need of the Mexican, despite the fact that this talk, talk, talk goes on in the Mexican family, goes on at work, in the cafés, and everywhere, there is always talk and more talk with endless friends." *Psychology of the Mexican: culture and personality* (Austin: University of Texas Press, 1975), pp. 17-18 y p. 26.

[53] pp. 40-42.

[54] *Iberomérica*, pp. 257-58. (Use of masculine pronouns above does not exclude women; it only avoids stylistic awkwardness.)

thinks it is more exact to speak of the Spaniard's personalism, or personal absolutism).[55]

The antithesis between Spaniards and Protestants is now a cliché, going back to at least the 17th century. Protestants developed the social value of work and a profession, and made wealth an ideal, and work a virtue . . . Luther exalted work itself as a divine service . . . Calvin took this attitude to its extreme: for him economic success leads to God and opens the doors to heaven . . . Consistent with his ideal, the Protestant considers that time is money. The Spaniard, to the contrary, who has made generosity one of his virtues, will always feel disposed to kill time.[56]

From the above one can see that the Hispanic—let us say Latin American—work ethic involves a different concept of time, which coupled with the absolutist concept of the person, justifies spending time in conversation.[57] The person does not have to change, but simply wait and converse:

the man who converses and waits, giving to conversing—the sacrament of conversation, today in decline—all the dignity of the human word, and while waiting, the infinite background of hope.[58]

Galo Plaza, former President of Ecuador, former Secretary to the UN, and man of letters, refers to the Latin American emphasis on contemplation instead of action, and a concept of time opposed to the Anglo-Saxon saying, "time waits for no one."[59] Galo Plaza in the same passage also refers to a recurring sense of time in connection with the Quechua verb for "to be," which means "to stay put." Thus, a concept of time opposed to the Anglo-Saxon "time is money" seems to come from both the indigenous and the Spanish or Portuguese sides. In sum, Anglo-Americans feel that they need to justify their existence by working, thus their worth tends to be quantified. On the other hand, talkative Latin Americans feel in no hurry to end a pleasureful

---

[55] Rosenblat, p. 51.

[56] pp. 48-49.

[57] Castro, *La realidad histórica de España*, p. 309.

[58] Rosenblat, p. 51.

[59] *Latin America Today and Tomorrow* (Washington: Acropolis Books, 1971), p. 23.

conversation. The right to exist is already granted by the sheer fact that one is a person—whose value cannot be quantified. Work is simply a necessity for some, but it does not dignify. [60] One saying in Spanish referring to work is, *"Si el trabajo es saludable, que trabajen los enfermos* (If work is healthy, let the sick work)." Another is, *"Si el trabajo fuera cosa buena ya lo hubieran acaparado los ricos* (If work were a good thing, the rich would have already monopolized it)."

The close connection between *personalism* and *verbalism* is still apparent in the traditional elitist and verbalistic curricula of Latin American universities. Humanistic education is more verbalistic than scientific or experimental. The positive side of having studied the courses in this type of curricula is the prominence in public life of those who have studied law, or philosophy and letters. The negative side is that the verbalistic tradition makes it difficult to bridge the gap between theory and practice. For example, a graduate engineer, because of his education and continuing disdain of manual labor, will not be the first one to pick up a tool in the field where a job is in progress. Some think that this aversion to working with one's hands is disappearing. Nevertheless, the following observation is still valid: "As soon as someone is in the position of giving orders, he resists picking up a tool or operating a machine, unless it is a robot, or an enormous and impressive piece of machinery."[61]

The separation between theory and practice is seen also in legalistic, yet dictatorial governments. Spain was an extremely civilized and lawful nation during the colonial period.[62] The letter of the law had to be respected. Three examples of legalistic concern over the years can be cited: dictators who still legalize their coups, the *requerimiento,* a legal instrument used during the Conquest, and the legal formula used to receive some of the Crown's new laws with the phrase: *"se acata pero no se cumple,"* meaning that it is respectfully accepted but not enforced. Preoccupation with the law is revealed in the importance of the *licenciado* (lawyer), and the verbalistic manifestations of this preoccupation are evident in the term *leguleyo,* the lawyer who resorts to legalistic arguments that he barely knows himself, to convince others of the correctness of his point of view. The person who has *el don de la*

---

[60] Rosenblat, passim.

[61] Havighurst, p. 61.

[62] Lewis Hanke, compiler, *Latin American Civilization* (2 vol., Boston: Little, Brown, 1973), Vol. 1, passim.

palabra (the gift of speech) is powerful, because the word can alter reality. The following remark seems to confirm this assertion: "Latin American emphasis on diplomacy and courtesy tends to make us value the word more than the deed and to think that resolutions constitute action."[63]

Examples of the complementary relationship of *verbalism* and *personalism* abound. The heroes of Latin American novels and movies, unlike their U.S. counterparts, are not the "strong silent type." Talk is even more incessant in Hispanic American *telenovelas,* or Brazilian *novelas,* than in the U.S. *soaps.* Moreover, the topic of conversation is about people. The Latin American would rather converse than read, because in conversation one is in intimate contact with other persons. In every instance what counts most is the human contact, which solidifies one's innerworld. [64]

The two cultural traits discussed here have not favored social cohesion on a broad scale, nor aided in material progress. Latin Americans interpret reality through persons. The support of what they say is dependent on an interpersonal reality, which permits them to be unconcerned with statistically based scientific proof. The imagination is thus free to improvise from one's interpersonal experience, to elaborate as convincingly as possible the verbal structures that affirm one's self. In doing so, Latin Americans avoid being driven directly by the quantifiable measures of time and money. Living is uppermost. Perhaps this is what Latin Americans mean when they say: *"Hay más tiempo que vida* (There is more time than life)."

The Role of Women in Latin America

The way in which women relate to their reality, and to men within this reality, is one of the most definitive traits of Latin American culture. This is true especially in comparison with women in the United States, where today in many circles a very strong feminist movement is taking place, in which, U.S. women, with impassioned expressions of solidarity tinged with leftist ideologies, confer on themselves the responsibility of liberating their *Latin American sisters* from the yoke of *machismo* and *imperialism.* However, the latter, if they are poor—without denying the existence of *machismo,* or male

---

[63] Galo Plaza, pp. 23-24.

[64] Rivera, p. 6.

chauvinism, and without being necessarily revolutionary—first think of liberating themselves from poverty in collaboration with men. If they are from the upper, even from the middle class, they are aware of the advantages that they have, stemming from their family and class position, aside from knowing that they are morally superior and influential, precisely because they are women, favored by a feminine solidarity developed many years ago, long before the height of the feminist movement, and before it provoked a reaction to what some consider the imposition of a political orthodoxy, called *political correctness.*

The following comments are based on notes taken from readings done before the last decade, and on my own experience—more than 42 years of marriage to a Latin American. I will not try to deal with the most recent data from an ever larger bibliography, a practically impossible task. I only intend to offer some notes and reflections on relations between men and women in Latin America, while contrasting them with their counterparts in the United States. I offer them for whatever they are worth, without attempting to avoid opinions that cannot help but come from my own circumstance.

When comparing Latin and North American women, class differences must be taken into account. For example, among men in the United States, one finds chauvinistic attitudes just as extreme, or more so, than those of Latin American *machismo.* With certain reservations we could postulate that *machismo,* or male chauvinism, stands out more in the lower class of both cultures. Perhaps this prominence explains the rather generalized idea that women in the United States are more emancipated than women in Latin America. This idea rests not only on strictly cultural considerations—the basis of advantages and disadvantages on which women and men relate to each other—but on how much the situation of Latin American women approaches the model of the United States. This model stems from a higher socioeconomic level and a supposed equality between women and women, which calls for the elimination of the notion that that they have different roles. Many Latin Americans, both women and men, are opposed to eliminating their distinct roles. Moreover, neither are they ready to equate the economic privations of poor women with *machista* oppression, although this equation has suited the revolutionary left. This does not mean that the two cannot co-exist, in which case they complement each other to make life harder for poor Latin American women; however, the error lies in equating poverty with *machista* oppression in every case.[65]

Even Latin American women who are poor support each other through a network of relatives and women friends, a support that is lacking for many North American women, for example, single mothers, abandoned in great urban centers or in rural shacks. Latin American middle and upper class women, although they may not be able to avoid the responsibilities of the home, indeed can afford to have domestic service, available only to the very rich in the United States.[66] On the other hand, U.S. housewives, even during the *feminist revolution*, must themselves take care of the cleaning, cooking, marketing, and the children's transportation.

In light of what has been said above, one cannot deny that socioeconomic factors influence the way men and women relate to each other, or the degree and persistence of male chauvinism, both in the United States and Latin America. However, there are attitudes on the part of men toward women, and vice-versa, that go beyond socioeconomic boundaries. An example is what happens in mixed marriages.

Among those of us who know both the culture of the United States and that of Latin America, the opinion seems to prevail that marriage between a North American man and a Latin American woman will have more chances of lasting than the contrary. Why is this so? The North American man will likely make fewer demands on his Latin American wife than she would expect from a Latin American husband. Marriage of the latter with a North American woman is more problematic. Here both parties' demands on each other overlap. She will demand more freedom and authority of him than he is used to

---

[65]"U.S. women see machismo as the basic sign of Latin women's oppression and impotence, interpreting the signs of their own cultural prejudices; this, and other erroneous concepts and the attempts to transfer them, seem to indicate that 'women's liberation' North American style will not work in 'more traditional' societies." Ann Pescatello, compiler, *Hembra y macho en Latinoamérica* (México, Editorial Diana, S.A., 1977), p. 22. (The translation from Spanish of this quotation, as well as the one that follows, is mine.)

[66] "As opposed to the common U.S. woman, the Latin American woman (especially the woman from the middle as well as the upper class) can afford to have domestic help; therefore, she is more free to develop her talent in public life, while maintaining a certain image and dignity among the members of her family." Pescatello, p. 17.

granting, whereas he will expect her to tolerate male behavior that the Latin American woman is accustomed to view as normal, or inevitable, as, for example, physical infidelity, though the husband may behave discreetly and continue to provide economic support. To understand the attitude of so many Latin American women, one must see it against the backdrop of the support structure provided by the extended family, or its substitute, a network of women friends.

On the other hand, an example of how socioeconomic status may affect a Latin American woman married to a North American is seen in the problems of adaptation that an upper, or middle class woman has when she tries to become a model North American housewife. She must do without domestic service, although she has all the modern household gadgets. On the other hand, a Latin American woman from the lower class married to a North American (a less frequent case) is delighted with the convenience of the newest gadgets. Her economic status is bettered drastically. However, even a Latin American woman from the lower class may miss the relatives of the extended family and her friends. In certain aspects, in Latin America, she is not as alone, nor as dependent on her husband (at times, in the case of passing, or illegitimate unions, this dependence never existed) as is the suburban housewife in the United States.[67] The fact that the Latin American woman—in Latin America—may be willing to accept the double standard of the man's sexual infidelity, and also if she is poor, illegitimate children, economic insecurity, including physical mistreatment, must be viewed in the light of the support given to her by her relatives and friends. Of course no Latin American woman likes her husband to be unfaithful, but she does not think of taking revenge by doing the same thing. Besides, she prides herself on being respected. She simply understands the man as he is, how he functions in a system. If she lives in the United States, she may see his behavior in another way. Moreover, married women of the middle and upper class not only have the support of the family and friends, but also a security—though it entails restrictions voluntarily respected—granted them by their fulfilling a well defined and respected role in their society.

---

[67] A friend of mine married a Mexican servant, who undoubtedly could not adjust to the solitude of a married woman in a California suburb. Divorced after two years, she, however, opted to remain in the United States with people of her class and culture.

Of course there are Latin American women who do not accept the role of wife and mother, or the role of the unmarried daughter, aunt, or cousin. However non-conformity exacts its price, dividing women into two groups. This dichotomy brings about *social casualties,* in that the ones who do not conform are relegated to the role of easy women, prostitutes, mistresses, concubines, or women who for different reasons do not have a permanent relationship with just one man. The respectable unmarried woman who does not live with the family, but rather alone in her apartment, is not seen often, or certainly less often than in the United States. For example, a television program like the *Mary Tyler Moore Show* in the 70's would have had little success in Mexico. Nowadays there are many *telenovelas* (similar to the U.S. soap operas, yet different in that they finally come to an end) in which independent women appear, but, in general, their sexual behavior is a source of great dilemmas. In the *telenovelas* one does not find the lighthearted and carefree solution of the *Mary Tyler Moore Show,* that of an independent young woman who manages to have friendly relationships with men without letting it go any further, easily avoiding all masculine intentions to have sexual intimacy. Or, if perhaps there finally is, the viewer never knows, or cares. Anyway, she continues to be independent and respected, professionally and socially, free from all the moral restraints imposed by the family on a respectable, although professional, single woman. In Latin America, roles unlinked to the family, even by the persons who fill them, do not enjoy the same approval as in the United States.

According to many U.S. women, men are to blame for the strict moral code imposed on Latin American women. However, they fail to understand that Latin American women themselves demand it, because it gives them areas of security inexistent for the former. It also brings the above-mentioned *social casualties*, the roles relegated to the *fallen*. It allows and perpetuates as well the *double standard* of sexual behavior, overly exemplified in Panama, according to the following quotation:

> *La querida*—the mistress—is found on all social levels, from the policeman or Zone laborer who tries to support two or three women and their children to the aristocrat who proves his masculinity by eloping with every lower-class Queen of the Carnival who proves willing.
>
> The traditional seclusion of upper-class girls until marriage, the unbridled liberty of the their brothers, and the existence of a large underprivileged group have made the *casa chica* (little house) a widespread institution in

Latin America. In colonial Panama, men . . .went . . . in search of premarital and extramarital adventure. Many of them recognized their illegitimate children and this gave rise to the large number of lower-class families who bear the same surnames as the aristocracy. Marriage was traditionally arranged to suit the parents'convenience; romance was found elsewhere if it did not happen to coincide with marriage. In theory concubinage has always been condemned by the Catholic Church; in practice the local clergy has done little to enforce this disapproval and in fact counsels patience and resignation on the part of wifes [sic] . . ..

The *querida* is a prestige item, like the Cadillac. Men flaunt their mistresses, take other men to call on them, provide them with luxuries usually far more expensive than those they give their wives. Panamanians boast, 'We do not hide our mistresses like the Costa Ricans.' *Queridas* are the subject of gossip at the market and in the park; everyone seems to know all about such relationships and to tolerate them. It is generally agreed that a man has a right to as many mistresses as he can afford."[68]

Regarding the causes of the double standard, among them the protection of daughters, an Arabic and Iberian heritage, we should remember the theme of so many Golden Age Spanish plays by Lope de Vega and Calderón that deal with a man's honor. His honor depended upon the *opinión* of others. It came from outside. It was enough for one to suspect that the wife was unfaithful, or that the fiancée was not a virgin. Whether the husband believed that his wife was unfaithful was secondary. In an extreme case, in a work by Calderón, *El médico de su honra,* the husband has his wife killed, although he knows that she has not been unfaithful to him, only because others believe it. Octavio Paz cites the following sayings regarding the need to avoid any possibility of a woman's going astray: "A woman's place is in the home, with a broken leg" and "Between a female saint and a male saint, a wall of mortared stone."[69] The existence of a numerous class of poor people coupled with the attitude of Latin men that they can continue to do what they did during the Conquest and the Colonial period—make women their own—perpetuates prostitution.

Women who do not conform to the strict standards men impose are obligated to assume disgraceful roles separated from the family. There

---

[68] Lewis Hanke, *Modern Latin America: Continent in Ferment* (Second Edition: Revised and Enlarged, Princeton: D. Van Nostrand Company, Inc., 1967), Vol. I, pp. 188-189.

[69] Octavio Paz, *The Labyrinth of Solitude,* p. 36.

is an intermediate ground between the one occupied by the decent women, the wife and mother, and that of the fallen woman. Latin American men, believing that this ground is one that corresponds to *gringas* (North American and, in a broader sense, foreign women), do not classify them as decent women, and thus consider them easy prey, which becomes evident in the way they treat them. Furthermore, Latin American women agree with the men. They sharply criticize what they think is the loose behavior of *gringas*, and they stifle any hint of envy, or desire to emulate them, by adhering even more closely to traditional sexual morality. They do not criticize the men as much. They behave as expected. How should they behave, if not like men? Women are the ones who are responsible. In other words, women are the first to criticize those who stray. Even those who have not succeeded in adhering to the standards of traditional conduct—in which they must be the virtuous one—criticize others and themselves in accordance with those standards. Moreover, women from the lower class, once they are able, emulate upper class ideals of behavior. Herein lies their hope for legitimacy, an important goal, involving among other considerations, the need to have their illegitimate children receive their father's surname.

An anecdote about the legitimizing behavior of a mistress is appropriate at this point. Her behavior received the approval of women from the aristocracy, since it conformed to values of the class that expelled her, or to which she never belonged. The wife comes to the mistress' house to insult her and to tell her to leave her husband. The mistress, assuming the wife's role—the legitimate role—answers that here she is the *señora* (lady). According to the lady who told me the story, the roles were reversed, in that the mistress behaved like a lady and the wife like a floozy. Although the mistress herself has not succeeded in belonging to the upper class, her children have, or will. They in turn eventually can incorporate her. I know personally several people who were born as illegitimate children, and who now have been accepted in the same class as their father. What has likely helped them to be accepted is the legitimizing behavior of a mother who emulates, as much as possible, the values of the class in which she aspires to see her children.

The following points summarize the reasons for the separation of women into two classes, whose poles are the *self-sacrificing woman* and the *prostitute*. Written more than fifty years ago about Mexican women, applicable in many aspects to women of other countries even today, they exemplify *machista* attitudes now condemned by the feminist movement:

1) A woman, regarding her ability to defend herself, is born with a constitutional inferiority because of her sex, because of her *opening,* a wound that never heals, unlike a man, whose defense lies in *not opening up.*
2) *Modesty* is a woman's defense.
3) A woman, considered to be an instrument, must fulfill the roles imposed by men, as a keeper of certain values in the role of prostitute, goddess, great dame, lover, transmitter and treasurer—but not creator—of values that nature and society attribute to her.
4) A woman must be protected (or protect herself) at every moment against men. Let us remember the Iberian and Arabic attitude expressed in the two sayings cited earlier: "A woman's place is in the home, with a broken leg" and "Between a female saint and a male saint, a wall of mortared stone." (Today many Latin American women still believe that it is the woman's responsibility to protect herself, if she is not protected already, by not exposing herself to the dangers of the other sex. If she does, she must accept the consequences.)
5) A woman is hieratic, dark, reserved, and passive; her instincts are those of the species, an impersonal essence, and not her own.
6) A woman is a symbol, which represents the stability and continuity of the race; her function is ensuring that the legitimate order, pity, and sweetness prevail. Therefore she is due respect.
7) A woman is exposed to all dangers.
8) A woman converts her weakness into virtue, hence the myth of the long-suffering and consequently virtuous woman (and thus morally strong, in this sense stronger than a man).
9) A woman through suffering becomes hardened and insensitive.
10) A woman, as an enigma, attracts and repels; she is the image of fertility and death. Does she think? Does she feel? Sadism begins as vengeance in the face of feminine inscrutability, and as a desperate effort to get a response from something one fears is insensitive, because, as Luis Cernuda has said, "desire is a question for which there is no answer."

Octavio Paz develops his theory on the dichotomy of attitudes towards women in Mexico, by alluding to the worship of the Virgin of Guadalupe (Tonantzín) and to the indigenous people's rejection of masculine gods after the Conquest. The Virgin of Guadalupe becomes the protector of orphans. Hence the reverence paid to mothers, which is expressed in so many ways, as in, for example, the following speech from a Mexican film: "Your father may be any son of a bitch . . . . Your mother you have to respect . . . You only have one." On the other hand, the preoccupation with the mother has its negative counterpart that gives rise to expressions in which precisely one fails to respect the mother. The prime example is *"Tu madre* (Your mother)," or the complete version, *"Chinga a tu madre* (Fuck your mother)." Another is *"a toda madre* (at full mother)," meaning "at full throttle." Perhaps the worst insult is for a man to say *"Yo soy tu padre* (I'm your father)" to another who is not his son. It implies that the former has possessed the latter's mother. Thus she is a *fallen* woman, like Malinche, who let herself be violated by surrendering to Hernán Cortés. Hence Malinche has become the symbol of the violated mother.[70]

The Family

One can gather from the previous section that many of the traditional values of Latin American culture are related to the family, the institution that has so much influence in the lives of women and men. The family determines how they should relate to each other in an ideal moral plan, in which until now more responsibility falls on women than on men. At this moment, I do not propose to resolve this question, but rather take up another, the extended family versus the nuclear family.

There are those who insist that the extended family in Latin America is a myth, that now large families of several generations living in the same home do not exist as before, if in fact as many ever existed as believed. Also they point to the large percentage of illegitimate unions among the poorer classes, for example, the cases of a single woman with three or four children of different biological fathers, and who at the moment lives with another man, whose economic support is meager, or totally lacking. The number of extended families (outwardly patriarchal, yet matriarchal in their daily functions) compared with the total number of families of the entire population has probably never been very large. After all, extended families, though historically larger, and perhaps proportionately more numerous, come from the

---

[70] Paz, pp. 35-40..

aristocracy, which is by definition a minority. Neither can one deny the large number of couples in free or unstable unions. However it is not simply a question of statistics—the quantification that U.S. sociologists and economists like so much. It is not just about the percentage of illegitimate, or legitimate unions, or about extended families of several generations compared to nuclear families with father and mother plus one or two children. A great variety of family structures exist in Latin America today, just as they do in the United States. Undoubtedly the relative number of nuclear families has increased, but the psychology of how family relations are viewed reveals the historical influence of the extended family as a source of values emulated by persons who are not necessarily members of an extended family, or of the aristocracy. Moreover, in Latin American inns and tenement houses many people adopt—to the extent that it is economically and morally possible—the roles of mutual responsibility customary in the traditional extended family.

A series of factors related to the extended family in Latin America spring into view, whether they are seen as causes of its existence and perpetuation, or as consequences of the cultural values it has handed down. First one should consider that the extended family arose out of necessity, to implant, expand, perpetuate, and preserve Iberian culture in a new world populated by indigenous peoples, who, in general, were not expelled and eliminated, but rather slowly incorporated through a gradual process of *mestizaje* (miscegenation). This process involved primarily the union of indigenous women, then *mestizas* (women of mixed Indian and Iberian parentage), black women, and afterwards *mulatas* (mixed black and Iberian), mainly in Brazil and on the Caribbean coasts, with Spanish and Portuguese men. Iberian women arrived to retard the process, to be legitimate wives, take charge of the servants of the patriarchal Spanish and Portuguese house, and to educate the *mestizas,* who were incorporated legitimately into Iberoamerican society as acknowledged daughters or wives of Iberians of lesser rank, or in fact as servants and concubines. Since there were more Iberian men than Iberian women, the indigenous women, and above all the *mestizas*—desired first for their sex and then considered more valuable because they were more industrious and capable of being educated, an ability and predisposition inherited from their indigenous societies—adapted to Iberian culture sooner than *mestizo* men. Unless they were sons of very important people, of a *conquistador,* such as Martín Cortés, or of an indigenous princess and a

Spanish captain, such as the Inca Garcilaso de la Vega, in general, *mestizo* men were incorporated in the society of other *mestizos,* separated from indigenous society, subordinate, yet over the years more and more inclined to emulate Iberian society, the society of their fathers.

Without doubt herein lies for many well-meaning people, and advantage-seeking ideologues, the patriarchal character of Latin American society, implanted by the sword and the rape of indigenous women, then perpetuated on an unjust economic basis through structures, among them the extended family. These structures subjugated, and continue to subjugate the poor, the *mestizos* and the indigenous for the most part, and women, who are dominated both by poverty and men. The well-meaning people I mention, mainly from the United States, forget, or are indignant about the frequently voluntary participation of indigenous women and *mestizas* who lived with and married Iberian men, thus joining the society of the *father.* These well-meaning people do not comprehend Latin American culture, though they think that they do. In addition, there are the ideologues, who may understand the culture, but who hope to take advantage of muddy waters.

Let us not simplify too much. The culture of the *father* was imposed with the help of the wife, the Iberian educator and administrator of willing and cooperative pupils in the space of the home, where the presence and values of women are felt today at every step. Anyone who is really familiar with Latin American culture knows that in many aspects it is profoundly feminine, in that women have played an extremely important role since the beginning. They have known how to devise defenses as, for example, turning to other women, in a feminism begun long before the one trying to liberate them. Their feminism does not exclude men, because they know with whom they are dealing, and are less ideological and more realistic than some U.S. women. Perhaps I say this because I am a man, but in general, it seems to me that Latin American women feel more sure of themselves, of being women without hesitation, as demonstrated by what a Chilean writer, Pía Barros, said, when, after her talk, she was asked about the feminist movement. Her answer, from a Latin American feminist, similar to others I have heard in a variety of ways, surprised her U.S. interlocutor, when she said that she was happy to have a vagina. On the other hand, she emphasized the need for equal pay for the same work, and that the poor—men as well as women—must work together to free themselves from poverty.[71] A similar attitude—which reflects the point of view of a Latin American woman on questions of feminine liberation, not only under the specific conditions in Latin America, but also in the United States—was expressed by Cristina Saralegui, the host of a daily television program in Spanish addressed to Hispanic viewers in the United States.

> In order not to be left behind and to address Latin women in a stunning manner, Cristina created her own formula. The equation is one of her favorites. 'I like to say that liberation of Latin women is from the neck up, and not from the neck down, and that the most important organ that a woman has is between her ears, and not between her two legs.'[72]

What is evident in both comments is a feminism of modern Latin women, which has a face unlike that of U.S. feminism, because it is based on values generated by the family, a feminism that while seeking justice for women and men does not try to eliminate their differing roles.

Extended families in Latin America, from the beginning of the Colony, while allowing the process of *mestizaje* and acculturation to occur, slowed it down, as a measure of security, because they were a minority surrounded by Indians and blacks, in addition to their unincorporated descendants of mixed blood. They did it by means of arranged marriages among Spanish, or Portuguese families—later *criollo* families—of the same region, to the point that first cousins, whose parents were also first cousins, married each other. Thus the regional economic and family interests of the dominant class were protected by permitting them to reconcile their concern over the *purity* of the blood line with the scarcity of Iberian women and men's habitual unbridled sexual behavior, and the *blind eye* that was turned upon accepting as one's legitimate wife an Iberianized *mestiza*. Slowing the process of *mestizaje,* a process still incomplete to this day, gave more time for *mestizos,* also Indians, in direct or indirect contact with the dominant *criollo* class, to assimilate and emulate many of its values. We can imagine that as a *shadow* class of the other, *mestizo* families

---

[71] The talk mentioned above, followed by questions and answers, took place at Lewis and Clark College, Portland, Oregon, in the spring of 1991.

[72] Diana Montané, "Más cerca de Cristina Saralegui," *Más*, Vol. III, No. 4, julio y agosto, 1991, p. 44. (The translation from Spanish is mine.)

came to exist (or individuals who adopted family roles), which, as far as possible, emulated the customs and reflected the attitudes of the aristocratic *criollo* families. Today the dividing line between original *criollo* families and the upstart ones is blurred, as regards economic power and the degree of *mestizaje,* but the values generated by the former have remained, with regard to the responsibilities of family members and the desire to emulate them. This is true not only of the professional, middle class, but also of people living in the popular inns and neighborhood tenements, who confer upon themselves the responsibilities of mother, daughter, aunt, son, brother, or father, besides the religious responsibilities of godfather or godmother and those of friendship.

Some of the consequences of Latin America's traditional family values have been pointed out above, for example, the double standard and the dichotomy of *decent women* and *floozies.* Others, which I wish to point out below, the same as those already mentioned, are derived from the insistence on maintaining well differentiated and defined roles for men and women, in a cultural context that demands more self-denial and responsibilities of a woman, in her being a good daughter, mother and wife, than of a man, whose responsibility seems to be limited to his being the family titular head, protector, and financial provider. However, to meet this responsibility ideally, he must finish his career in order to be able to get married and be ready to support his wife and his children in a lifelong commitment. On the other hand, as for his sexual behavior, no one thinks of demanding that he be a virgin when he gets married. After he is married, he should respect his wife, and it is hoped that he will not cause a scandal. The Latin American wife, on the other hand, with the support of family and friends, does not expect a perfect husband who will give her everything. Her expectations are unlike those of the U.S. housewife isolated in suburbia, away from her family, which was not large in the first place, and who does not feel the same obligations towards a daughter or niece. She is a realist and abides by a lifelong relationship, in which not only the husband, but also the children play a role. Children are a mother's consolation, her occupation, or her main concern, which does not stop when they become adults, especially if they are daughters.

Between mothers and daughters, and among Latin women in general there seems to exist a support system, and also a feminine predominance—we could say a matriarchy—in the home, the market, and, of course, the convent. Since long ago, as said before, they have not needed formal feminist associations as in the United States. Let it be said in passing that formal associations, with programmed activities are more a part of Anglo-Saxon than Latin America. One notices in Latin America more separation of the sexes. An extreme case is the one noted in an Argentine rural setting, similar to one in U.S. Kansas in the 19th century. At a dance the separation of men and women is categorical, until finally the men suddenly make their move and join the women with an aggressive attitude that is accepted, though not completely reciprocated.[73] Just as in the home and the market the feminine influence predominates (not to mention the convent), men get together and converse in bars and cafes. They too support each other more in Latin America than in the United States.

Through the years I have noticed that in the United States the solitary couple, a man and a woman, separated from others, or perhaps in momentary contact with other couples from the office—passing ships for the occasion—who get together in clubs or bars. Later, when married and living in the suburbs far away from their families, they demand everything of each other in a *meloromantic* idealism that cannot be fulfilled, or in a disappointed or egotistical predisposition, now in style, to demand everything of each other. And if it does not work out, they get divorced, thus teaching their children—who are scattered—not to get married, just live together. Latin women learned about simply living together, but by necessity, before North American women did. When able to do so, they have abided by the values of the class that, according to them, taught them about the importance of family stability, or the stability offered by friends, because there was no other.

The large family during the colonial period and the unstable and anarchic years after Independence has served not only as a cultural bastion for the Iberianized classes, the Peninsulars (before Independence in Hispanic America), and the *criollo* minority. Also, extended family members with their network of friends, settled in the same region, have provided protection and security in countries where until today one seeks to solve problems preferably through a relative or friend, before turning *without any pull* to impersonal, and bureaucratic institutions of the state, plagued by bothersome procedures. Without well-connected relatives or friends, a person of the subordinate class

---

[73] Ezequiel Martínez Estrada, "Los pueblos," *Radiografía de la pampa* (Buenos Aires: Babel, 1933), p. 93.

who wanted to get into the upper class sought the help of the godfather, and the boss, or landlord. Looking for security and stability through the family's personal connections has accentuated regionalism insofar as its members do not consider living permanently elsewhere, far from relatives and friends. Regionalism, coupled with the lack of mobility and failure to get beyond family and local interests, has delayed the political stability of many countries, as well as the just and efficient operation of institutions that work without the *lubricant* of personalistic and arbitrary influences.

At this point it would be opportune to interject two rather typical examples of how family and regional connections have had an influence in the lives of two Central American friends. They studied at universities (or colleges) in the United States, and then returned to their respective countries to get married and become fathers. Without even thinking about the possibility of moving to another city, much less to another country, they have devoted their lives to sedentary positions. One of my friends bought, or had his house built, in a kind of family colony, next to the houses of his wife's brother and sisters. The children have settled in the same city, if not in the same neighborhood. My other friend and his wife have had houses built for their four children and their families on the land belonging to the main house.

Of course, at times Latin Americans are forced to move, even go to another country for economic or political reasons. The emigration of those with few economic means is carried out suddenly and under precarious circumstances. However, if possible, the emigration is not permanent, and is done through family contacts in the country of destination. For example, men from certain poor Mexican families, many times from the same *pueblo,* come one after another to certain parts of California and Oregon to work a couple of years. One sees cases in which the male members of some families have made the *pilgrimage,* as if it were an initiation rite for the families in the Mexican *pueblo* from which they come.

Social Class

It is helpful to treat in more detail, and with the support of other opinions, the relationship of the family with social class, especially the problem of forming a middle class before the prestige of aristocratic *criollo* values, and the desire to emulate them. Although the following quotation is based on observations carried out before the year 1967, it still reflects the conservative attitude of many middle groups.

> The well-intentioned attempt to identify a liberal, industrious, frugal and reformist middle class in the present Latin American social structure is destined to early facile success and eventual catastrophic failure. There are groups which have the superficial characteristics of the middle class; they even talk, write, and think of themselves as being middle class, but objectively they are not, and it is hard to see how they can ever bridge the distance which separates their intrinsic conservatism, their respect for hierarchical values, their admiration for their natural aristocracies, their overwhelming desire to rise and be accepted by those they regard as their betters, from the dynamic reformism which is usually associated with middle-class idiosyncrasy.[74]

With reference to what happened several decades ago, although it seems that it is repeated today, the author of the previous quotation comments that the leaders of the so-called middle class—or of the middle groups—were reformists. However, when they got closer to political power through the popular vote and the industrialization following the Second World War, the middle sectors became very rich:

> No apparent contradictions developed between the aristocratic landowner and the wealthy radical leader: on the contrary, they became fast friends and political colleagues once the rising bureaucrat had bought land and racehorses, joined the local country club, and taken his first golf lessons. Thus in a relatively brief period of time, the violently outspoken reformist leaders of 1938 became the sedate, technically minded, and moderate statesmen of the 1950's . . . The leadership of the urban middle sectors had gained access to the very sources of political power which they now shared with the traditional landed aristocracy . . .. In Latin America there survives what is perhaps one of the largest and oldest aristocratic establishments in the Western world.

The author cited refrains from censuring the intellectuals for being adaptable:

> Most of the continent's intellectuals are in opposition and have adopted a quiet but forcefully critical attitude. There are extremely few writers, poets, musicians, economists, architects, or historians of the last generation who are willing to identify themselves with the political and social arrangements

---

[74] Hanke, pp. 174-75.

made by the leadership of the urban middle sectors. This does not mean that they are all members of the Socialist or Communist parties.

However, he sums up the problem of forming a middle class that has its own ideology and actions with the generalization that "social climbing has become a political institution." He contrasts what he calls the emotional and intellectual isolation of the middle groups, their cultural sterility, with the middle class in Europe, which did not look for a guide in the aristocracy, or in foreign influences.[75]

To confirm the difficulty, if not the failure, of the middle groups in forming a middle class of their own, due to their adoption of aristocratic values, another voice is added: "Thus, in contrast with the middle classes of other areas of the world, Latin America's metropolitan middle class seems to have not yet developed the desire to save, or to have yet reached a peculiar class ideology."[76]

Now many readers will object that Latin American society is changing, that this quotation and the ones before are old, from the 1960's, and that in Chile, Argentina, Uruguay, Costa Rica, parts of Brazil, Venezuela, and Mexico, the middle class not only exists, but is more and more numerous, above all in the Southern Cone and in Costa Rica, the model country of Central America. Certainly the percentage of people who belong to the middle groups has increased, a class which, according to the previous quotations seems to constitute a middle class. For example, the percentage of salaried employees such as office workers who live from one payday to another may have increased. But one must ask first if their mentality has changed. Then, if the following events do not indicate the emergence of a middle class conscience: the Cuban and Nicaraguan revolutions, the election of Salvador Allende in Chile, the leftist movements in Uruguay and Argentina, aside from the guerilla struggles in El Salvador and Guatemala. We know that many of their leaders have come from the middle groups.

With regard to the first question, I believe that the mentality of the middle groups has changed very little, although they are more numerous today than 30 to 35 years ago. For example, the problems that plague Argentina—which has no reason not to be a very prosperous country—are due precisely to the great number of middle

---

[75] Hanke, pp. 176-77.

[76] Havighurst, p. 74. (The translation from Spanish is mine.).

level salaried persons, who apparently demand privileges of the State that are enjoyed by the *señores:* the ranchers, the industrialists and the military officers. The salaried also want to be *señores.* Their aim is to belong to an elite. As for the second question, I do not believe that the revolutions, or national socialist struggles indicate the emergence of a middle class conscience like that of the U.S. Let us take as examples the North American *liberal* and the Latin American socialist revolutionary. I maintain that in their attitudes and behaviors they are not the same person. Many times their rhetoric coincides, they support many of the same causes, they think that they understand each other, but really do not. Each one speaks with the interlocutor he imagines. The North American *liberal* still considers that he is from the middle class, although according to some conservatives he has begun to demand too much of the state, but he still believes in it, although he bitterly criticizes it. He wants to continue appealing to his institutions without using personal influence. He believes that institutions should serve others the same as him—but no more. He doubts more and more that institutions are as efficient as they should be, but he still wants to modify them, not destroy them. He does not ask for a *fresh start* in his own country. Here is the inconsistency, since with regard to certain Latin American countries, he does support the revolutionaries. He believes—or perhaps *believed*—that by supporting the leaders of the *national socialist revolutions* the *people* would be freed from poverty (supposedly everybody except for a few intransigent oligarchs), and that effective institutions would be established under leaders, perhaps a little authoritarian, but just and egalitarian, who think like he does. Besides, by means of this revolutionary process, Latin American women would be freed from *machista* oppression. He is deceiving himself. In general, leaving aside the rhetoric, the cultural mentality of the Latin American socialist revolutionary is opposite that of the North American *liberal* on every point mentioned.

Aristocratic Attitudes

To begin this section I want to relate several anecdotes, or personal observations. My circumstances allowed me to meet a Latin American lady of a generation before mine, whose attitudes exemplified the mentality of the aristocracy of her origins, which had suffered material losses. Her attitudes were rooted in her social class, the surnames of her ancestors and those of her husband, in the purity of blood line, in tradition, which went back to the metropolis, the Spain of her ancestors, and to the adopted metropolis, the United States. Further, they were rooted in her knowing that she was a lady (*señora*), wife and mother, distanced from the "rabble" around her—although she had to feel charitable toward the destitute—in short, in a self-sufficient aristocracy that did not depend on money.

When I traveled to Mexico City for the first time, by bus and at nineteen years of age, a *pilgrimage* taking more than a week, I met Armando, a young Mexican, who invited me to stay at his parents' home, where I remained for more than a month before becoming independent enough to move to a boarding house. Armando's father had a radio station. I remember that Armando had to go to a small room across from the bedroom, where he worked as an announcer—a chore for him. For me it was a privilege for which I envied him, because I still did not have a total command of Spanish. They told me that I did not say enough when speaking, or responding to a question. On the ground floor of the house, always cool and somewhat dark, one of the radio announcers would have breakfast with me—*café con leche* (coffee with hot milk) and *pan dulce* (sweet bread) that crumbled into a thousand pieces. I hardly understood him because of his rapid production of staccato syllables, separated by what sounded like only single and double "R's." I remember that each morning he would eat a *mango* stuck in a special fork, and that he cut it with a knife into slices, which he ate with another fork. Or was the same one? Anyway, I believe it was at the first breakfast that I became familiar with this fruit, which I tried to eat the same way. It was not until later that I learned about the figurative meaning of *mango,* the one that is not masculine, but feminine, although it ends in "o."

One day while I was walking along the street with Armando—near his house, because I still had not gone alone anywhere—I must have wanted to show off the feminine *mango,* by applying the word to a girl, who for me was very pretty. The problem was that the girl I admired was an Indian, or *mestiza,* from the lower class. I remember that she was passing in front of a gasoline station. Armando's mother was Spanish, from Andalucía, and Armando's father, was of Spanish descent with very little *mestizaje,* if any. "But that girl is an Indian," said my host. That comment has stayed with me all my life. Later, he seemed to disapprove less categorically of another girl, who had a darker complexion than the "Indian" near the gasoline station. Perhaps it was because the second girl, despite being a Mexican of humble parentage, was from the United States, and spoke English. I have wondered what could have been the reason for his change of attitude, perhaps my protests, or his disappointment at having tried to correct what for him was the egalitarianism of a naïve *gringo*.

A year later, established as a resident at a boarding house, one day I understood why I should not sing the French song *La mer* so soulfully. (*Lamer* in Spanish means *to lick*.) I did not make another blunder in this way, but in another. I invited one of the servant girls to the movies. By chance, my friend, José Luis, saw me. He is the brother of one of the Central Americans mentioned earlier. As a person from the upper class, because he is the son of a Guatemalan diplomat (as a child he had lived some nine years in Germany), he had the expected social graces, and as a friend of mine felt obligated to suggest to me that my going out with a servant was in no way suitable. His criticism was not based on racial discrimination, but on the servant's class, on her lack of education. Her skin tone was lighter than his.

It is not that race is totally ignored, but it is a secondary factor, used only to confirm or deny the others. For example, due to historical reasons, in most places it is not strange to see a person with dark complexion who is poor and badly dressed. On the other hand, a poor, barefooted white person, like some I have seen in Costa Rica, would attract attention in El Salvador, Guatemala, or Nicaragua. Yet, the dark skin of a well-dressed man, obviously a professional, is not important, or less so today than it was before. It should be noted also that together with white skin, one not only expects the person in question to be well dressed, but to also have a good education. Therefore, well-meaning North American university students who arrive in Latin America poorly dressed, through carelessness, lack of concern for formality, or a desire to identify with the poor, offend both the latter and the oligarchs, particularly if they walk around barefoot, and then put their dirty feet on the furniture. The North Americans who supported the *Sandinistas* were called "*sandalistas*" (sandal wearers) in Costa Rica. Apparently the Costa Ricans felt that wearing sandals, coupled with wearing shabby clothing, is the next thing to going barefoot.

Another personal observation of class discrimination comes from the criticism expressed by a Mexican American of humble parentage, who had received a university education. She identified with her Mexican heritage, but not with the lower class, certainly not with the way the *pelados* of Mexico City speak Spanish. Although they were of humble origins, her parents had not given her the *pelado's dejo* (accent), and she wanted to avoid the way of speaking of the capital's lower class. She also did not think it was right for her friends to speak that way. That is why she protested strongly when a North American friend of hers, who had learned Spanish very well, came back from Mexico speaking like a *peladito*.

In the summer of 1944 I worked in a pea cannery in Milton-Freewater, Oregon. There I met several *braceros* (Mexicans workers brought to the U.S. under an arrangement with Mexico), and even worked with them. In 1948 I saw one of them quite by chance when I was walking with a Mexican lawyer along an avenue in the very heart of Mexico City. I greeted the *bracero* warmly, and stopped to talk to him for a while. The lawyer felt very uncomfortable during the conversation, and later commented to me that he thought it strange that I should know a *bracero,* and that it was not suitable for me to continue having anything to do with him.

I worked during 1950 for the U.S. Department of Agriculture in a joint campaign with Mexico to eradicate the hoof and mouth disease. A Mexican and an American worked together as livestock inspectors in a specific sector that we had to cover each month. For reasons of security, because peasant farmers had killed some inspectors at the beginning of the campaign, two cavalry soldiers escorted us, since we had to travel on horseback due to the lack of roads. My partner was from a well-to-do class of a provincial city. The soldiers were of from the lower class, although one of them was married, and had reached the rank of sergeant, a position that for my Mexican partner allowed him to behave too much like an "equal." The sergeant was not "of his class," or "of his condition," also a phrase so often used to discourage a young woman, or man, from marrying a partner of questionable background.

To close this section on aristocratic and elitist attitudes, I should mention, though no longer directly as personal experience, the influence during the first part of the 20th century of José Enrique Rodo's essay *Ariel*—now forgotten by many. In it he extolled the aristocratic spirituality of the character Ariel as opposed to the lustfulness of Calibán. Without Rodo's having intended it, other Latin American authors—in the movement called *Arielismo*—took Ariel as a symbol of spirituality and the superiority of Latin American culture opposed to Calibán, who symbolizes the materialism and vulgarity of U.S. culture. I commented earlier that one suspects—rather has to admit—that in the country of Calibán there is much of Ariel. The author of the essay would not have been opposed to this assertion, objecting to the all too easy schematism of Ariel/Latin America versus

Calibán/United States. Be that as it may, Rodo's essay, which almost nobody reads now, and which many do not know by name, despite having felt its influence, reinforced the aristocratic attitudes of Latin American culture.[77]

Greater Latin Community

The above heading does not indicate any intention for now of exploring the mutual influences, present and past, of the Latin community, as, for example, the French from the 18th century, or the Italian in Argentina and Southern Brazil. Such an intention would require an entire book. However, the fact that certain Latin American cultural characteristics transcend their borders stuck in my memory when I learned of several comments about the French by a North American professor at Harvard. It struck me that the characteristics mentioned coincided with those I had observed in Latin Americans, so much so that I am taking the liberty of using the comments of the Harvard professor to support my own observations. First one should point to the transcendence of Latin culture, which becomes even more obvious when contrasted with Anglo-Saxon cultural characteristics. "The French [let us say Latin American also] love to generalize. Even on topics about which they know nothing. [However] they generalize establishing distinctions." Let us remember what was said about Latin American *verbalism*. The French [just as Latin Americans] stress differences, categorize, and classify. According to the Harvard professor, North Americans tend to unite separate elements. This should be contrasted with Latin American separatism—an Iberian heritage that we have seen earlier. Politically separated, but warm in their personal relations—with relatives and friends, and others from the *patria chica* (hometown, or region)—when they start to converse they stand closer to each other than North Americans. The French do the same thing. Consequently, as regards how Latin Americans see their neighbors to the north, the latter seem cold and dull in their manner.

The following and final quotation from the Harvard professor, which seems to describe a Latin American characteristic, should provide a transition to the next section: "North Americans are deeply convinced that mankind tends to want what is good. The French are

---

[77]See Note 25 earlier in this chapter.

educated with the idea that from others one can expect the worst."[78] The same thing occurs with Latin Americans. Just as, or even more than the French, they view the world with undeceived eyes.

Conspiracy Theories

Latin Americans boast of their shrewdness, of their being undeceived, of not trusting strangers, and of resorting—if necessary, since others do it—to dissimulation, even deception in order not to be fooled. In the case of the *mestizos*, above all, not believing in strangers and taking advantage of a moment's luck to benefit themselves and their own is mandatory. They lived initially between two cultures, not belonging fully to either one. They have seen their hopes of a better life dashed so many times, in countries that have had too many governments, in the extreme case of Bolivia as many as the years of their lives. Resorting to dissimulation and deception is to be intelligent. There is a saying in Spanish involving alliteration of the letter "b," *"Bueno y bruto se escriben con la misma letra,"* which expresses the point. It could be rendered in English as "good and gullible are written with the same letter."

Distrust reinforces the personalistic attitude of only depending on the family, on friends, or on the *caudillo* of the province, whose grandiloquent rhetoric enthuses some at moments to later disappoint. In a world where the leaders and their projects seem Adam-like, without the firm basis of precedent or continuity, bursts of enthusiasm may be great, but only momentary and sporadic.[79] More and more one trusts members of the family, friends, *compadres* (co-godfathers), and cynically gets from others what one can, knowing everybody does it.

Only with an attitude like the one I have just describe, was I able to comprehend the reason for theories on Kennedy's assassination—to give an example—that I heard in El Salvador in the summer of 1969, during the war of this country with its neighbor Honduras, the so-called

---

[78] "Les français épinglés," *l'Express*, 1-7 August, 1977, pp. 54-56. The comments come from an interview with Laurence Wylie, a professor at the University of Harvard. (The translation from French is mine.)

[79] I owe my use of the adjective *adánico* (Adam like), referring to Adam in the Bible, to the Chilean writer and literary critic, Fernando Alegría, who uses it to characterize the Latin American protagonist of his novel *Camaleón*.

soccer war. One of my in-laws, seconded by many others, assured me that "Johnson had Kennedy killed." Today, in the United States few believe in the report of the Warren Commission's official investigation, but I have not heard my compatriots say that a president of ours would be capable, like a Roman emperor, to *do away* with somebody, like a Mafia godfather. A North American—perhaps naïvely—resists believing such a thing. On the contrary, Latin Americans always seem ready to attribute the worst motives to the actions of others, especially those of the leaders, the *generalones* and *chafarotes,* pejorative names used in El Salvador by the civilian oligarchy to refer to the uncultured, corrupt military officers, who are needed and despised.

I remember that the mere suggestion that Johnson had Kennedy killed provoked in me a reaction of shock, anger, and disbelief. How could they imagine such an act of a man with the ability to become the president of the United States, a process that presupposes an earlier consistent and prolonged effort, based on morality, on good. How could such a person commit such an immoral act, without any mitigating circumstances? ("He knew how to pull it off?") I wondered what the relation was between morality and the performance of one who holds a position demanding responsible actions. I have not been able to find a satisfactory answer. I know from what has happened between 1969 and now (still without blaming Johnson) that no one believes that Oswald acted alone. It seems strange that Jack Ruby could have killed him so unexpectedly, and that later he also died without testifying. It would seem that I am now saying that my in-law and other Latin Americans who think like him were right. "There is something fishy here." They are only partly right. I believe that there is still an important difference between the mentality of thoughtless suspicion and that of total naïveté.

It is important now to elaborate on what was said at the beginning of this section regarding the Latin American experiences that have created distrust, disappointment, and cynicism. Political instability in Latin America—although it has not been as extreme everywhere as in Bolivia—would cause the Latin American to believe what my in-law relative said about Johnson, because he equates him with repressive and bloodthirsty dictators like Trujillo of the Dominican Republic, Estrada Cabrera of Guatemala, Rojas Pinilla of Colombia, or Pinochet of Chile, to mention a few. We can go back to the Colonial period, to Lope de Aguirre, who took command of an expedition down the Amazon. He did it by killing successively almost all the others before finishing the expedition. So it is that for many Latin Americans there are numerous examples of strong, capable men who have had others killed. One must remember that the Indians and the *mestizos* need to achieve their goals by being submissive, impassive and astute. *"Más vale maña que fuerza,"* for which the Oxford bilingual dictionary gives "Brain is better than brawn." However, one must add that *maña* means *artifice, shrewdness, adroitness,* and *cunning.* Complementing the Colonial experience is the example of the Spanish *pícaro* (rascal, or rogue), who comes from the 17th and 18th centuries, the period of Spain's decline. He manages to eat any way he can, unlike the famished *hidalgo* (nobleman), (like the one already seen in the 16th century in *El lazarillo de Tormes*), whose pride obliges him to dissimulate his poverty, and to not work. Be it through deception, or dissimulation, both the *pícaro* and the *hidalgo* lie. Thus it should not surprise us that Latin Americans suspect that one should not believe what is seen on the surface.

Latin Americans' tendency to suspect that there is a conspiracy, to not believe what they are told, to look for some hidden meaning, is revealed in their taste for plays on words, which consist precisely of an obvious meaning and another hidden, malicious one. Extensive use of plays on words called *conceptismo,* one of the characteristics of the baroque literature in the colonial period, coupled with *gongorismo* (decorative and obscure verbalistic complication that overuses metaphors and hyperbaton) is noted in contemporary writers such as Alejo Carpentier, Miguel Angel Asturias, José Donoso and Julio Cortázar. They, among others, enjoy creating complex, torturous, and indirect verbal puzzles.

> The Hispanic American [Latin American] taste for the most elaborate and difficult forms, for the most cultured and artistic forms of expression, not only is evident in its literature and art, but also is reflected in everyday life and even in popular art. Its popular poetry is baroque, syllogistic and fond of the conceptual and cryptic. The popular singer frequently composes using forms as elaborate as that of the *décima* (10-line stanza).[80]

Verbal Masks, Walls, and Patios

The improvised verbal duels of the *payadores* of the Argentine Pampas, and of the harpists from Veracruz, Mexico, allow each singer to impose his person, surpassing his opponent's resourcefulness with even more elaborate forms and cryptic conceits. Thus, before the other,

---

[80] Uslar Pietri, "Lo criollo en la literatura," p. 72.

he compensates with loquacity for any disadvantage he may have, real or imaginary. He can "carry him between his legs," to translate the Spanish *"llevar entre las patas,"* by insulting him in a veiled manner, while concealing himself through pretending to be innocent. The insult is found only behind the obvious, the effect of which the other has to dissimulate. When the latter returns the insult, the former in turn must pretend not to have noticed, because if he does, a fight would start in which knives would come out.

The *conceptista* verse (which involves a conceit, or a play on words), a tricky and malicious question, and polite expressions used not to offend or be offended before others, may be considered verbal masks, ways of not communicating. Yet people talk a lot, perhaps realizing that they are not communicating with each other, or possibly as a compensatory effort to impose themselves more by their enthusiasm and the way of saying things than by what they say. They talk to convince without letting themselves be convinced, as was said earlier. The effort to affirm oneself with words is seen in animated conversations held at what seems to be an intimate distance, from the North American point of view. They start after the obligatory greeting, the handshake or embrace between men, and the kiss on the cheek, given more in the air, when women greet one another, or between women and men who know each other. In passing it should be known that traditionally a woman, when about to shake hands with a man, extends hers in a *feminine* way, as if he were going to kiss it. People talk about everything and nothing, "about the wisdom of the rooster and the immortality of the crab," to literally translate *la sabiduría del gallo y la inmortalidad del cangrejo*. The day's events are recreated verbally, and at the *sobremesa* (at the table after dinner) all the adventures and vicissitudes of relatives and friends receive comment. In the cafes and bars the country and the world are set right, or they are given up for lost. "The situation in El Salvador is hopeless. The only solution would be to take out all the Salvadorians and put other people there." Because people talk so much—one hears bits of gossip, foolish remarks, jokes, confessions, exaggerated and abundantly detailed anecdotes, plans improvised at the moment, which fly through the air like so many other unfulfilled possibilities, plus the grandiose projects elaborated upon in grandiloquent speeches—all this verbal activity creates a structure that is reality in appearance, and at the same time a mask, or barrier. It incites a bombardment of words to impose another possible reality, another fiction, another mask, that in a constant beginning constructs another castle in the sand that will be erased anew by the first waves.

Verbal masks serve to cover up, dissimulate, and build up hopes in warm contacts with relatives and friends. The high stone walls that surround houses and patios, keep the activities of the people one trusts from public view. They are a defense against *"la calle* (the street)" —the outside world of strangers, and against those of *"otra condición,"* meaning another class. Outside the walls, as another defense that replaces them, contact among strangers, with the public, tends to be distant, lacking in kindly smiles, unlike the superficially friendly treatment given to strangers in the United States. In this country one does not usually raise walls around houses. Middle class people have their patio—rather, their front yard—open. Enclosing it with a stone wall would seem an insult to many, closing oneself off from the neighbors and the public. Besides, the open yard is an almost obligatory display of the owners' level of prosperity and diligence.

No, walls are not needed, and North Americans are kind to customers in stores and markets, because their defenses are others. One of them—kindness *for the occasion*—because of cultural differences, which we will see in the following chapter, disconcerts the Latin American, just as it does the Frenchman in the following quotation:

An American meets a Frenchman who is visiting the United States and immediately invites him to dinner at his house. The Frenchman is ecstatic: How open and hospitable the Americans are! The following week he will see this American again, who may not even recognize him. Or he will see this American everyday for two years and their relations will not change.[81]

---

[81] "Les français épinglés," p. 58. (The translation from French is mine.)

Chapter Three

The Third Road

Stereotypes: Origins and Significance

Stereotypes are the result of the conflict between the ideal image that a culture has of itself and the image it creates of another, based on incomplete observations. Stereotypical images are formed about the second culture, normally judged by the specific behavior of a few individuals, like that of drunken and rowdy sailors just off the boat. They are based on a set of ideal values of the first culture. In these stereotypes, which are almost always unfavorable, more than one true element is exaggerated and generalized.[1] The tendency to generalize, and the consequent exaggeration through omitting details, seems to be an innate mental process in humans. Also it is humanly impossible for one to be totally objective in appraising a different culture, because of the subconscious ideas and beliefs inherited from experiences living in one's own. Even if people believe that they are conscious of the ideas on which they base their appraisals (certainly they have more control than they think), their conscious opinions appear tinged by unnoticed

---

[1] On writing these lines I have incorporated what Lewis Hanke says regarding stereotypes in *Modern Latin America, Continent in Ferment* (2nd. ed. New York: Van Nostrand Reinhold Company, 1967), Vol. 1, p. 188.

suppositions. It should be added that the difficulty one has in judging another culture objectively, does not stem alone from the influence of one's own. Also, the judgment of any individual regarding another culture tends to be subjective, because contact with it is short and superficial.[2]

Nevertheless, a certain degree of control can be exercised. If it is not, as is usually the case for the reasons mentioned, and if in addition, the stereotypical attitudes that individuals of one culture have regarding another become inflexible in the face of new evidence that refutes the preconceptions supporting these attitudes, they now border on prejudice and fanaticism. In the following lines I will try to separate stereotypes, preconceptions, prejudice, or fanaticism, because it seems to me that all arise from the contact of some members of one culture with another. They can be differentiated in that stereotypes and preconceptions, placed on a scale from positive to negative, despite being negative most of the time, would remain closer to the center than prejudices and fanaticism. What all of them do have in common, besides their roots, is that they offer a method—a *road*—for the person who is interested, to get to the bottom of a culture's values through how it expresses itself about another. Finally, they offer a *road*, traveled personally, that validates my own experience, reconfirming, perhaps synthesizing, the appraisals of Latin American culture made in the first two chapters—in the antithetical *roads* of variety and unity.

It is very easy to judge foreigners wrongly, because—besides their different customs, which can upset our values, making us defend them through stereotypes and prejudices—they cannot express themselves in our language. They seem dumb. I remember the many times in Mexico I seemed tongue-tied when trying to express an idea. I have observed the same thing with North American students in several study programs in Latin America, not only their difficulties in expressing themselves, and the impression of inferiority they must have left, but also the misunderstandings caused by their not understanding what was said to them.

There are several other factors, aside from those of language, that hinder understanding between two peoples, perpetuating the tendency of both to use stereotypes as a defense mechanism, in order not to feel

---

[2] The subjectivity of any opinion is seen in the popular saying: "Cada uno habla de la fiesta según le fue en ella (Each speaks of the party according to how it was for him/her)."

bad before the power and success of the other culture. Mexicans, for example, although they may come to admire *"gringos"* (North Americans) for their organization, their power, and technical development, cannot easily forget that the *"gringos"* stole half of their national territory, which for them is an unforgivable injustice.[3]

Unfortunately, some people still harbor racial prejudice, happily less than before, exemplified by the comment of the infamous *Billy the Kid*, a hero in more than one Hollywood film. Before Bill Garrett sent him off to the other world, the beardless murderer boasted of already having killed twenty-one men (one for every year of his life), not counting *Mexicans.*[4]

Deep and irreconcilable cultural differences can exist between two peoples. Although anthropologists and linguists instill in the study of their discipline that every language and cultural custom is suitable and adequate for its practitioners, one is not Eurocentric to think that at bottom, despite the adequacy of all languages for their native environment, some are incapable of dealing with the *world,* and that there are certain customs we find intolerable. For me these are, among others, infanticide and mutilation of the face, or any other part of the body. Further, I could never bring myself to enjoy eating the eye of a roasted goat, which some consider a choice morsel.

Stereotypes of the *Gringo*

When one says *gringo,* it is already known that one is dealing with stereotypes of the North American, developed from the Latin American cultural perspective, and for the reasons discussed earlier. The presentation of a series of *gringo* stereotypes is done to illustrate again, and reconfirm, what was said in the previous chapters about Latin American cultural values.

The first example, transcribed below, is not mine, but rather given by Robert B. Mead, Jr., an expert on Hispanic culture. Translated from Spanish into English, I read it to a class of North American university

---

[3] *"Gringo"* in Mexico, in Central America, and some countries in South America is used as either a familiar or pejorative name for the North American. In Argentina it is applied mainly to Europeans. Its meaning in this country and others of the Southern cone is broader.

[4] Jorge Luis Borges, *Historia universal de la infamia* (5a. ed., Madrid: Alianza Editorial, S.A., 1981), p. 71.

students largely unfamiliar with Latin America. After I finished they remained silent, which made me think they were offended. In this thought I was perhaps mistaken, but not in their feeling that the text referred to them. Trained in self-criticism, the half-truths had the result of the popular saying: *"La verdad no peca, pero incomoda* (It's the truth that hurts, or literally, the truth doesn't sin, but makes one uncomfortable)." They were upset, if not offended, and none of them laughed. On the other hand, each time I have read the following description to Latin Americans, they have burst out laughing:

> The majority of North Americans are slaves dominated by their high standard of living, to which they pay an almost blind homage; they are controlled by their big business and financial interests; they are die-hard materialists without any understanding of aesthetics and refinement in life: art, music, philosophy, and literature. They all live in luxurious houses, enjoy all the modern comforts ever invented, and when they travel through another country they judge it according to the excellence of its sanitary installations, the availability of food sufficiently antiseptic (and tasteless one could add) for the delicate North American digestive apparatus, and the exactness of its public transportation schedules. Their family life is centered around and governed by the children (all spoiled), and the majority of the decisions are made by North American women. Sports mean more than education. And it would seem, North American tourists are born with chewing gum in their mouths, dollars in their pockets, a camera in their hands and dark sunglasses on their noses.[5]

A few comments need to be made on the above stereotype, though they will be brief, because more examples are coming. First, going back to the students' reaction, although they may have recognized as true some parts of the description—their high standard of living, their food with fewer spices, their punctuality, the importance given to sanitation, and even their dress, their dollars, gum and tourist camera—this does not mean that they are ready to change their behavior, or accept the cultural bases from where the criticism is launched. Most of them do not understand—although they may accept as a fact, perhaps well deserved—that their high standard of living can seem ostentatious to so many poor Latin Americans, or that, on the other hand, it is not accompanied by aristocratic good taste that dictates that one should season food well, forget about so much punctuality in

---

[5] "Imágenes y Realidades Interamericanas," *Cuadernos Americanos* (nov.- dic., 1973), p. 41. (The translation from Spanish is mine.)

order to converse with one's friends, pay less attention to the material things of the bathroom, and more to the things of life, and that one should not wear clown-like clothes, nor hide behind dark glasses, and above all, not chew gum constantly like a cow. The camera, though intrusive and indiscrete, is perhaps least objectionable. But it is carried and used by reporters, who are not normally aristocrats, also by tourists, who should try not to look like they are, if they want to be good ambassadors.

Mead's description carries other messages discussed before: North American materialism vis-à-vis Latin Americans' refinement and understanding of aesthetics, the Arielist thesis, besides their firmer authority over children, and the maintenance of traditional family roles, an authority that has not been diminished by the imbalance coming from divorces, and women who are too liberated.

To finalize these comments and present another series of stereotypes from my own experience, of which I became aware through feeling at times that I was the stereotype, let us note once again that *Calibán* (the United States) has built fabulous libraries and patronized symphonic orchestras, theaters and great art museums. As happens in all criticism, *"se ve la paja en el ojo ajeno y se deja de ver la viga en el propio* (literally, one sees the straw in the other's eye and fails to see the beam in one's own)." However, for what it is worth, it should be heard.

The Truck Driver Gringo:

This negative expression—which I have heard in El Salvador from people who consider that they are of the aristocracy—emphasizes the lack of good manners of the North Americans they have known. Because most of them are white, the same as Europeans, high society accepts them, but culturally and socially it looks down on them. Nonetheless, since they do not have any Indian blood, they end up being *good candidates* for young marriageable women.

The Naïve Gringo:

Very generalized among Latin Americans, above all among Mexicans and Salvadorians, this stereotype paints the North American as naïve, off guard, candid, lacking in shrewdness, slow, and easily deceived. It is due to his simplicity and frankness, his direct behavior without refined manners and the delicate tactfulness demanded by *proper society*. His laconic and dull way of speaking contrasts unfavorably with the Latin American's verbosity and effusion. Being naïve does not mean that the North American is stupid, but in its most negative connotation, it carries the seal of disapproval. The Latin American recognizes the North American's ability to organize; he admires and envies his wealth, but, as said before, he feels superior in the spiritual sense, considering that his neighbor to the north is a Philistine. Here again attitudes appear that are rooted in the *Arielist* school of thought, except that the persons who expressed this stereotype of the *naïve gringo* had never read, nor heard of Rodó's essay.

The *naïveté* of the *gringo* from the Latin American's perspective can be attributed to his seeming to accept what he is told with less suspicion. Moreover, unlike the Latin American he does not immediately resort to tricks to get what he wants, behavior that I have observed personally in rush hour traffic, and when having to stand in line. The Latin American does not stand in line if he can avoid it. He turns to friends to let him go directly, leaving others waiting, to the ticket or teller window, the office, or the key person, and if he finds himself in a traffic jam where his friends cannot help him, he vents his frustration by leaning on his horn. The *gringo,* on the other hand, waits patiently, refrains from honking, and even fails to take advantage of narrow lanes, or those that unexpectedly open up, where a Latin American motorist would pass through in an instant.

The North American, if it is possible, wants to follow the rules, because he basically believes in them. They have served him well. But for the very reason he believes in them, he does not make them complicated. To cash a check in any bank in the United States a person usually goes to one window, at most two. On the other hand, in Mexico or Costa Rica, the personalistic behavior of the customers is combated—their habit of looking for a way to avoid steps through influential contacts—with superorganization and an extremely complicated series of procedures. This is the other side of the coin. Now I laugh at my own naïveté of thirty five years ago when I was willing to wait in line with everyone else at the airport in Guatemala, and I even became annoyed with my wife—from El Salvador—who had made arrangements with an official to let me through immediately. For her my willingness to wait with everybody was incomprehensible.

The Latin American, from his personalistic perspective calls the *gringo* naïve. In turn, the behavior of the former provokes the disapproval of the latter, because he does not see it from the same personalistic perspective. Personalism explains the behavior of the Latin American: his tendency to suspect a conspiracy, his tolerance for strongmen, his morality which seems to adhere to norms that are not those of the North American. Personalism, defined earlier as a tendency to trust relatives and friends first, before trusting systems and continuity, coupled with the Latin American's intelligence and energy, explain the phenomenon of the *Adam-like man* cited earlier.

The Latin American's experience has shown him that he is right in distrusting systems, because they have not worked for him. He finds himself in a vicious circle that is hard to break. He finds it extremely difficult to stop depending on personal relations, which were necessary during the Colonial period. It was indispensable for the less fortunate to establish a relationship with a boss and a good godfather, in the manner of the servant with the lord, or the squire with the knight, an arrangement of convenience between unequals inherited from the Middle Ages and continued in the Americas. Contrast the history of Latin America with that of the United States: more than two hundred years of continuity compared to the series of dictatorships in Latin America, even the failure of Chile, where the long democratic tradition, and the military's respect for civilian government was proclaimed.[6] Latin American political experience exemplifies the lack of continuity particularly at the national level—fragmentation of time as well as fragmentation of territories. Therefore systems are not trusted, but periodically one has to turn to military organization to establish order. Above all the tendency of taking care of oneself continues, and of looking out for the welfare of the family and friends, besides the tendency to admire the strong man and to tolerate what is convenient at the moment.

---

[6] In this "failure" the involvement of the CIA, the Central Intelligence Agency of the United States, cannot be denied, but to examine all the factors goes beyond the scope of this study. I recommend reading *El paso de los gansos* by Fernando Alegría.

The Easy Gringa:

As she is a foreigner, whose stay is usually not permanent, the traditional classification is not applied to her. She does not come under the category of a decent woman, because of the circumstances of her arrival as a Spanish teacher, often alone, unaccompanied by her husband or other family member. Thus, according to rumor or expectations, she must have come to have an affair with a *Latino*. On the other hand, neither is she considered a fallen woman, or prostitute. She is assigned a third classification, that of an *easy* woman.

The North American woman who arrives in any Latin American country today (for example a student in a university study program) is not to be blamed for the impressions left—rightly or wrongly—by those who came before. As an exotic and attractive woman, enigmatic if not easy, she immediately incites the amorous and aggressive attention of the young men, the envy of her *sisters,* and the concern, or disapproval of her *mother.*[7] I remember when some fifteen North American female college students moved into a boarding house in the Polanco suburb of Mexico City. The next day a great number of young Mexican men began to arrive, who, almost at any time of day, swarmed around the entrance like flies drawn to honey. The fiancées, or girl friends of these young men must have felt a bit jealous, or at least upset and worried about their suddenly being neglected because of those *güeras.*[8] And as for the concern and disapproval of Latin American mothers, I know for a fact that it is harder to place female students with families than it is to males, for whom they do not feel as responsible with regard to their sexual behavior.

The North American woman is not used to such strong and persistent male attention, which at times she does not know how to reject without offending, because often the attention does not come from strange men. Another thing is the *piropo* (verbal compliment, or comment) addressed to her on the street, or the excesses of some taxi

---

[7] Reference is made here to the daughters and the mothers of the families hosting North American female students.

[8] In Mexico one says *güero - a* to refer to a person with blond hair, often including any person who does not have black, or dark brown hair.

drivers.[9] In the first case she should think like Latin American women: assume that a man, even a best friend, may try at some moment to take advantage. Some Latin American men, certainly not all, imagine that they can take advantage of the credulity of the *easy gringa,* who arrives without knowing, or sometimes without wanting, to behave in manner that refutes the reputation that she already brings. Her ready and friendly smile, in situations in which a Latin American woman would look serious, is taken as an invitation, above all if she has allowed herself to be alone with a man—in the car, in the bedroom, or worse yet, on a bed, although she may suppose that they are, or demand that they behave, just like *comrades.* Latin women, when they hear stories of North American women who have placed themselves in these situations and later complain, react with the question: "And what did they expect? I—as man incapable of ever comprehending how a woman feels—am not the only one who asks this question. Although they may not agree, the most practical and succinct advice one can give them is that they should let themselves be guided by Latin American women, "who know what they're dealing with." The problem is that lately North American women—at least students in university programs—seem less and less willing to consult their Latin American *sisters,* believing that they are oppressed, and mistaken.

Now it is time to relate the *piropo* (that verbal compliment, which varies from being ingenious to being vulgar) to what a Latin American woman says about it. Her words summarize what I have heard on numerous occasions. "The *piropo* reaches the woman who lets it. A woman's smile indicates acceptance, and a invitation for more; protesting also indicates acceptance, and reveals that she can be reached. If she does not acknowledge a *piropo*, it does not affect her."[10] For the same reason I think that at the moment the *piropo* is expressed,

---

[9] I know of three specific cases: In the first, a man had his driver follow a North American female student who was walking along the street; from time to time he would get out of his car to expose himself. In the second, a group of North American women riding in a taxi noticed that the driver was masturbating, at which they indignantly, did the right thing to get out of the taxi immediately. In the third, a North American woman, at night, who was still in a taxi after her friends had gotten out, made the mistake of arguing with the driver over a double, though insignificant fare. He suddenly closed the door on her, and took her the next corner, who knows with what intention.

[10] These are the words of my wife, who was born and raised in El Salvador.

its author recognizes that he is not going to get anywhere. Aside from the fact that a man says it so that his friends can admire it, the *piropo* in a certain sense is a declaration that the woman to whom it is addressed is unreachable. In the best sense, it is an expression of admiration addressed to the woman, verbal gallantry, a *carpet* of words placed at the feet of the one passing. In the worst sense, it is a vulgar and dirty verbal hand, extended, but not dangerous, if she does not allow herself to be *touched* by it. The *piropo* is launched as a compensation, a recognition of frustration from not actually being able to touch the woman's beauty, only with words. But not even these reach her, because she—the Latin American woman—does not acknowledge them.

The Insipid Gringo, or Unsalted Potato:

A visiting professor from Spain teaching at a university in Portland, Oregon became angry one day at the inexpressive look on his students' faces. He pounded on the table and said to them: "You look like meat with eyes." I have told this anecdote any number of times to illustrate the contrast between North Americans' phlegm and Latin Americans' effusion. This contrast is partly due to the latters' verbosity and the formers' laconicism, but in addition to this difference go the latters' animated gestures and greater facial mobility. Moreover, to speak the Latin America's languages well, the facial muscles have to be more tense and move more, lending more expressiveness to the cheeks and lips, also to the eyes, eyebrows, and forehead. There is more: how the romance languages are intertwined with other factors, as we shall see below.

One hot summer day two Latin American women were bathing in a swimming pool at a U.S. university. Both were only about twenty-two years old. Thus it is understandable, in the light of Latin American men's behavior to which they were accustomed, that they were very surprised that none of the North American men bathing at the same time turned around to look at them. They complained bitterly, saying that the *gringos* had *horchata* (cold cereal drink) instead of blood in their veins. On that occasion they were not criticized for lack of life in their faces, but rather for lack of life in their veins, which for the two women, was the same thing. I must confess that one of these Latin American women ended up marrying a *gringo,* although for a long time she was going out with a Greek. Could it be that she opted for security?

A friend of mine, mentioned before, the one who criticized me for going out with a servant, when the time came to say goodbye, always said five phrases for every one of mine. I could not elaborate, did not know what more to say. Verbal effusiveness came to him naturally, together with the hearty handshake. Then it is right to call somebody an *unsalted potato,* if he cannot say more than four words and forgets to shake hands. It is not that I would forget to shake hands, but what I was able to say was never enough. Let us remember what was said before about verbalism.

Just as with greetings, the good-byes (or closing) in letters are long and ceremonious. An Argentine with whom I worked for two years in an office in Los Angeles noted that the letters that came to us from Mexico were formal and ceremonious, but warm at the same time, more so, according to the Argentine, than the ones from his country. In general, the North American does not react with the verbosity and effusiveness that is expected when given a gift, or granted a favor. Neither does he/she know how to react when Latin Americans offer him/her something. Good manners dictate that one should say "no, thank you very much," and praise what is offered effusively, because to accept it at first is not customary. One should wait for the offer to be made two or three times before accepting it, to be sure that it is made in earnest.

The most effusive, repeated, and sometimes ceremonious thanks should be given, when one is the beneficiary of a gift or favor. One time in Mexico when I was supposed to thank the hosts publicly for a program of folkloric dances and songs, I did not rise to the occasion. I thanked them, and tried to interject a couple of poorly chosen humorous comments. Above all, I did not succeed in elaborately praising the quality of the program and the courtesy of the hosts. I came up short.

The Obligatory, Automatic Smile:

In spite of what was said before regarding North Americans' lack of expressiveness, occasioning the nickname of *unsalted potato,* they do smile, but for Latin Americans it is an obligatory, fixed smile, put on automatically, whether they are happy or not. When their picture is taken, they have to show their teeth, or when they have to speak in public, even about things that should not make one laugh. Latin Americans are more honest in this regard, although they may dissimulate and defend themselves with polite phrases, as was commented earlier. They smile if they feel like it.

For the same reason that Latin Americans find North Americans' behavior dull, or insipid, because of their inexpressive facial expressions (in spite of the mechanical smile), insufficient gestures and laconic speech, the latter find the formers' facial expressions, gestures and verbal effusion too emotional and melodramatic. Tearful, gesticulative films and *telenovelas* paint an exaggerated picture of real life. When I was young, I found some Mexican films too tearful, and also too long. Today they do not seem so much so. On the other hand, it seems to me that my compatriots do not have enough liveliness in their expression, nor emotion in their relationships.

The Superior and Arrogant Gringo:

This is the image that many Latin Americans have, due in part to an inferiority complex, and to the fact that many North Americans indeed have a high-handed attitude in dealing with their neighbors to the south, because they know that they are superior economically and militarily. Some feel inherently superior, because they are white, blond, blue-eyed, tall, rich and powerful. The economic and military superiority of the United States is a fact that provokes mixed feelings on the part of Latin Americans, who feel that culturally they are different, and intimately superior to North Americans, while they envy, admire, and emulate them. They fear and pay homage to the North's economic and military power, while, at the same time, beating their breasts for their *malinchismo* (admiration of the foreigner).

On the other hand, many North Americans, influenced by the Latin American left (whose message comes to universities and churches, blaming U.S. economic and military policies for the majority of their problems), arrive in Latin America embarrassed and full of apologies. Some of them (groups sent by some evangelical sects, and teams from universities that before went to Nicaragua, not to speak of Peace Corps volunteers) actually go there to work with the poor. However, I would dare to say that most of the contacts North Americans have in Latin America are not with the poor, but with the middle groups and the upper class.

Program directors who send young North Americans to build latrines in Tijuana, Mexico (or elsewhere) are probably from the middle class, the same as those who will accompany them after work to have a beer, or to go dancing at a discotheque. The poor themselves will not be the ones to accompany them socially, although the young people have arrived with egalitarian ideas, plus others that are revolutionary. Moreover, I doubt very much that they stay with the poor that they have come to help, because the latter do not have the economic means to be their hosts. As for university and high school study programs, besides others exchanges, as, for example, those carried out between Costa Rica and Portland, Oregon, I definitely know that stays are arranged with middle and upper class families. Furthermore, despite egalitarian and revolutionary ideas, it is logical that cultural dealings and arrangements can be realized more easily between people of similar socioeconomic levels. Above all, despite what they may think privately, Latin Americans from the middle and upper groups normally are the first to seek and take advantage of contacts with foreigners. Although *yanqui* (North American) cultural imperialism has brought *rock* music and *blue jeans* to the lower classes, its members, generally, do not succeed in having as much social contact, be it with the arrogant *gringo,* or the one influenced by the Latin American left. The little contact they have will be as servants, tourist guides for the arrogant *gringo* on vacation, or as assistants of the North Americans building their latrines, who later go have a beer with the project manager, who perhaps is a law student from a well-to-do family.

The Generous Gringo:

However, there are ways through which those of the lower classes may improve their social status, although it is a long and painful process, and maybe one of the North Americans who have come to build latrines will indeed go have a beer socially with the poor assistant. For the same reason that the process of climbing is slow in their countries, many poor Latin Americans reject the path of revolution, dreaming instead of help from another stereotype, the *generous gringo.* They dream of going to the United States. Some fifteen years ago, a Salvadorian told me that he was coming to the United States by whatever means possible. In the meanwhile I do not know if this individual ever made it, but thousands of other have. Thirteen years ago, in a trip lasting over half an hour, an Ecuadorian taxi driver kept talking to me about the money he was saving to obtain a falsified visa through a *coyote*.[11]

I collaborated in bringing a Mexican boy, named Luis, to the United States. He was from the lower class of the capital, and his parents of meager means saw the chance to send him as an *adopted* son of a well-off North American couple. Before the couple's divorce, some ten years later, Luis, who was short and thin when he arrived, grew so much that I scarcely recognized him two years later. His family's sacrifice bore fruit, but perhaps only halfway, because of what I have learned since about the case. For a time things went well for the boy, but when he was older, Luis returned to Mexico where he worked as an interpreter, after some problems he had because of having brought one of his brothers. Later he returned to the United States, but he left again, this time as a deportee. Was his coming north a failure? I do not think so, because a process of social change was begun, or perhaps it was just continued, because his family in Mexico had already become urbanized, and had learned upper class manners.

While making the arrangements in Mexico, before bringing Luis, I remember that his family, despite its scarce means, hosted us in their living room, offering us, with the urbanity and protocol required for the occasion, one or two drinks. Their manners, and their courteous attention, to the extent that their economic status allowed, were already urbane, of proper, worldly society. Therefore, people like the those of that family, who are struggling to come up, do not understand why a rich North American wants to go around with torn trousers, or why a tourist from the North—I witnessed it—tried to bargain down the price of a toy of a poor street vendor. He was handicapped besides being poor, sitting on a small board with four wheels. He was asking for the equivalent of one dollar and fifty cents for his surprisingly ingenious mechanical toy, which for me was worth three times what he was asking, and in the United States ten times more. The North American woman began to bargain with him, either because she had been taught to do so in her high school Spanish class, or because she wanted to save half a dollar. The vendor was offended, and refused to sell it to her at any price. Good for him!

---

[11] Name used mainly in Mexico to refer to those who facilitate the entry of *Latinos* in the United States, normally by using false documents and exacting exorbitant prices. They are often worse than the one in the film, *El norte*, portrayed by Abel Franco, a friend and classmate of mine from many years ago.

The Gringo with the Sarape and the Charro Sombrero:

This lady's behavior is perhaps a sad and mistaken reminder of the last *gringo* stereotype that I plan to touch on, the stereotype of *gringos* wearing the *sarape* and the *charro sombrero* (*charro*: Mexican horseman, or cowboy) in Mexico, or sandals in Nicaragua. I am referring to North Americans who suffer from the *go native* syndrome, when what is expected, if they learn Spanish or Portuguese, is for them to speak like educated persons, and dress in an international fashion like individuals of their class. Many Latin Americans would have the right to protest as follows: "Don't disguise yourselves, don't lie, don't make fun, especially if we are poor, and don't ask us to start a revolution, because you're not the ones who'll get killed, or be tortured! We want what you and our rich have, by working, and if possible without killing each other."

Perhaps more reprehensible than the *gringo* with the *sarape* and *sombrero,* even more than the arm chair revolutionary, or the one in university classroom, are North American tourists who in their colorful and immodest garb want to shout to the four winds that they *"están" turistas.* But at least they are what they are.

Stereotypes of the *Latino*

On noting down the most common stereotypical images of the Latin American that one has in the United States, the very first thing that stands out, aside from a condescending attitude towards an inferior, is its vagueness and its failure to appreciate differences corresponding to reality. Ignorance and confusion complement each other. Mexico is south of the border, then come Panama and South America. All Latin Americans bring serenades, play the guitar, kill bulls cruelly, eat *tortillas,* and say *"olé"* when they dance. Five Central American countries do not even appear, and for the Caribbean, only Cuba and Puerto Rico exist. South America is jumble of countries, capitals, and geographic locations. Chile borders on Colombia or Venezuela, and Buenos Aires could be the capital of Caracas.

I will let the author of the stereotypical image of the North American—with which we began this chapter—continue. It should be remembered that the North American students became very serious when I read it, because they felt that it alluded to them. However, when I read the following stereotypical image of Latin Americans—just as exaggerated as the previous one—they burst out laughing, because it did not touch them personally, and as university students, they were aware of the intended irony:

> All Latin Americans speak Spanish, inhabit tropical lands, wear wide brimmed hats and clothing resembling North American pajamas; they avoid work whenever they can, take a siesta every time the opportunity presents itself (when they are not making love or dancing the cha-cha); they live in straw or adobe huts and their main foods are spicy dishes like "chili con carne," enchiladas and tamales; they start a "revolution" every two or three months, and, in general, they perform services and provide a picturesque background at the hotels, beaches and archeological sites that North American tourists love so much.[12]

The first impulse of Latin Americans—and mine—on reading the above paragraph is to establish differences by first removing the word "All," and adding that they also speak Portuguese in half of South America's territory. From there one would have to clarify that, in fact, there exists, for reasons that were explained earlier, an association between manual labor and the lower classes, and that consequently, people from the middle groups and upper class avoid it. However, this attitude towards manual labor does not mean that Latin Americans are lazy, or that they take a siesta whenever possible. What indeed can be gleaned from the criticism of their avoiding work and taking the siesta, is the Calvinist Protestant ethic of valuing work and material success. As for the rest, excepting the pejorative allusion to their making love, what the above description underscores with details that are true in some particular, is poverty, instability, the tropical and the picturesque.

Many Latin Americans resent seeing these points stressed, an emphasis that not only comes from ignorance, because once the clarification is made that not everyone lives in tropical lands, the same textbooks continue to promote what is strange, typically regional, and folkloric. A Brazilian professor used to complain to the graduate students in his class that the most widespread image of Brazil in other countries was that of the *Nordeste* (Northeast). Its peculiar characteristics marked by African influence were known abroad, while the enormous cities of São Paulo and Belo Horizonte, thriving commercial and industrial centers, besides the Europeanized Rio Grande do Sul, were ignored.

---

[12] Meade, p. 41.

The ignorant take note of external characteristics—the typical ones, which for them are exotic because of some incomplete and poorly understood experience—and then apply them without distinctions to all Latin Americans, creating a hodgepodge of *tortillas* eaten by Argentines, *tangos* danced by Cubans accompanied by shouts of *olé*. Scholars correct the external details and apply them where they belong. This is the process that I followed in the first chapter, or *road*. North Americans, and other foreigners, sorely need it, and Latin Americans justifiably ask for the correction of details. They do this out of the affinity that they feel for their country, and what is more, for their home region. In Ecuador they are proud to be Ecuadorians, but people from Guayaquil know that they are different, and superior to the people from Quito, and the latter feel superior to the former. This first *road* has no choice but to stress differences, or variety. But if we remain at this point, adding more and more details—underscoring what is strange and typical, which entails the danger of superiors wanting to help inferiors—we do not go to the heart of Latin Americans' mainstream culture. This culture comes from the Iberian Peninsula, and, in a process still continuing, and on a scale never attempted in other parts of the world, it incorporated Indians and black Africans—who speak Spanish and Portuguese. We do not get to the heart of what they think and feel in common, after they say, for example, "I'm a Bolivian, and you're a Paraguayan." Vis-à-vis North America and Europe they are both Latin Americans. To understand how they relate to each other, and above all, because of their history with the outside world, the second *road* has had to be the search for cultural unity, the antithesis of the first.

The third *road,* that of stereotypes, which I have traveled more in real life than in university classrooms and libraries, has led me to re-confirm—and attempt to synthesize—the common cultural traits of Latin America, having taken into account its differences. The main trunk of that common culture—of that cultural unity—seems to be of a plant extremely varied in its appearance, rooted in personalism and regional particularism, in the terrain of historical experience. It is grafted onto the physical and human geography of the New World, at the same time nurtured and exploited by the colonial metropolises, Spain and Portugal.

Other metropolises have followed; now they are the United States and Canada, Europe, and the international commercial enterprises. The confrontation of the Latin American countries with the new metropolises has reinforced Latin American personalism and particularism to the detriment of socioeconomic and political alliances. This is what I have been able to observe from the temporary perspective of my contact with Latin America, 1948 to the present, and my *personal circumstance* of having spent my childhood and adolescence in the United States. Paradoxically, the traits that unite Latin Americans culturally are the ones that divide them in other ways. But life—just as death—continues. On the optimistic side, and without falling into the error of making political predictions, one will have to see how the increasing international influence of popular music, of clothing, and of consumerism will affect Latin American culture. Latin America will remain open to outside influence, now that there seem to be more democratic governments, and authentic revolutionary fervor has subsided. Lately this fervor has evolved more into banditry related to drug traffic, and Maoist extremism on the part of groups like *El Sendero Luminoso* (The Shining Path) and the *Tupac Amaru* Revolutionary Movement. With time, influence from outside will become more intense, making young people in Latin America look more and more like their counterparts in the United States and Europe. I believe, however, that the changes will be more apparent than real. Analyzing the changes that are unquestionably taking place, and determining the degree to which they are substantial, will be the fourth *road,* long and hard, to be traveled another day. Today I will dismount here. My horse is tired.

INDEX